PELICAN BOOKS

ENGLAND IN THE
EIGHTEENTH CENTURY

Professor J. H. Plumb was born in Leicester where he
was educated at the University College and afterwards
at Christ's College, Cambridge. He began research
under Professor G. M. Trevelyan on the social structure
of the House of Commons in the reign of William III. In
1939 he was elected to the Ehrman Fellowship, King's
College, Cambridge. During the Second World War he
worked in a department of the Foreign Office. On his
return to Cambridge he became Fellow and Tutor of
Christ's College and University Lecturer in History. In
1957 he was awarded a Litt.D. for his work on
eighteenth-century history. In 1966 he was appointed
Professor of Modern English History at Cambridge, and
elected a Fellow of the British Academy in 1968. He
has written books on *Chatham*, *The First Four Georges*,
West African Explorers and *The Renaissance* and is the
author of *Crisis in the Humanities* (1964) and *The Growth
of Political Stability in England, 1675–1725* (1967). His
life of Sir Robert Walpole was acclaimed both in
England and America as one of the outstanding biographies of our time. He is now editing a multi-volume
History of Human Society. He was visiting professor at
Columbia University for 1960, and Ford's Lecturer at
Oxford University, 1965–6. He is the European
Advisory Editor for *Horizon*, the advisory editor for
history for Penguin Books, and editor of the Fontana
History of Modern Europe.

D0727030

J. H. PLUMB

ENGLAND IN THE EIGHTEENTH CENTURY

PENGUIN BOOKS

Penguin Books Ltd, Harmondsworth, Middlesex, England
Penguin Books Inc., 7110 Ambassador Road, Baltimore, Maryland 21207, U.S.A.
Penguin Books Australia Ltd, Ringwood, Victoria, Australia

—

First published 1950
Reprinted 1951, 1953, 1955, 1957, 1959, 1960, 1961
Reprinted with revised bibliography 1963
Reprinted 1964, 1965, 1966, 1968, 1969

—

—

Made and printed in Great Britain
by Hunt Barnard & Co. Ltd,
Aylesbury
Set in Monotype Baskerville

THE PELICAN HISTORY OF ENGLAND

To

MY MOTHER

CONTENTS

*

CONTENTS

PART III
THE AGE OF PITT

*

PART I

THE AGE OF WALPOLE

*

'I am no Saint, no Spartan, no Reformer.'

SIR ROBERT WALPOLE

CHAPTER ONE

THE STRUCTURE OF SOCIETY
1714–42

ENGLAND in 1714 was a land of hamlets and villages: its towns, such as it had, were on the coast. In Lancashire, the West Riding, and West Midlands towns of some size and substance were beginning to grow, but the majority of the population was still in the south and still rural. Estimates of population vary because the evidence is unreliable. Until the last decades of the century, it is largely a matter of intelligent guesswork. The population was probably, in 1714, about five and a half millions, and from 1714 to 1742, after an initial spurt, there was only a very small increase, but there were important changes in its distribution; East Anglia had a declining population; the West Country and South and East Midlands were fairly static, so was the East Riding and all of the north but Tyneside, West Riding, and South Lancashire, where the increase was marked; so, too, was the increase in the West Midlands. Surrey and Middlesex grew with London, whose rapid expansion of the late seventeenth century was maintained. These changes were due to the growth of towns and industrial villages. London exceeded half a million; Bristol passed Norwich and may have reached its 50,000 in this period. Manchester, Liverpool, Sheffield, Leeds, Halifax, Birmingham, and Coventry all ceased to be the sprawling villages they had been half a century earlier, although, as towns, they were small by modern standards, none of them reaching 50,000. Small as they were, they ate up men, women, and children and their population was only maintained, let alone increased, by a steady immigration from the country and in the north-west from Ireland.

The first noticeable thing about these towns would have been the stench. There was no sanitary system; an open cesspool in the court often served the richer inhabitants; the poor, as with Eastern peoples today, made a public convenience of every nook and cranny. The unpaved streets were narrow, often only six feet wide; at Bristol they were too narrow for carts, and sledges had to be used for moving goods. The houses of the poor were one or two room hovels, frequently made only of weatherboard with a pitched roof, placed back to back; or they were the houses of the rich, deserted because their owners were seeking more salubrious suburbs – ramshackle warrens of filth, squalor, and disease. Most cellars were inhabited, not only by people but also by their pigs, fowls, sometimes even by their horses and cattle. All tradesmen and craftsmen used the street as their dustbin, including butchers who threw out the refuse of their shambles to decay and moulder in the streets. About London and one or two of the large towns, enterprising market gardeners bought the refuse and the night soil to manure their fields, and this helped the growth of cleanliness.

All houses and cellars were desperately overcrowded – ten to a room was common in Manchester. It was reported that often the rooms were without furniture and lacking even beds; the occupants slept close together on shavings for warmth. Disease was rampant and unchecked: smallpox, typhus, typhoid, and dysentery made death a commonplace. A contemporary describes, in 1721, the way the parish authorities disposed of paupers' corpses in Manchester:

They dig in the churchyards, or other annexed burial places, large holes or pits in which they put many of the bodies of those whose friends are not able to pay for better graves; and then, those pits or holes (called the Poor's Holes), once opened, are not covered till filled with such dead bodies . . . How noisome the stench is that arises from these holes so stowed with dead bodies, especially in sultry seasons and after rain, one may appeal to all who approach them.

In the early part of the century, only about one child in four, born in London, survived; and probably the infant mortality was higher in the mushroom towns of the north. In the midst of death, the people sought palliatives and found them in drink, gambling, and violence. The consumption of gin – drunk mixed with fruit cordials – was prodigious, but largely confined to London, where it may have affected the death rate in the thirties, although virulent influenza epidemics also took their toll. Gambling was an antidote favoured by all classes of society; the wealthy favoured stocks, cards, and lottery tickets; the poor, crown and anchor, pitch and toss, or bull baiting and cock fighting. Violence, born of despair and greed, belonged to the poor alone. Most of the new towns were still, constitutionally speaking, villages; and they usually had no more than two parish constables to keep order. London, Bristol, Liverpool, and a few other large corporate towns were better off because they had resident justices who could read the Riot Act, but even their forces for keeping order were pitifully inadequate, and burning, looting, and destruction by the mob were commonplaces of life. And yet these towns drew an endless stream of emigrants from the countryside.

In London, which drew the most, conditions varied considerably. The eastern suburbs, Westminster, and parts of Southwark were as bad as the provincial towns. The area controlled by the City of London was better administered, although the social amenities were negligible. An attempt had been made to light the city in 1684. The lamps were shaped like frying pans and the fat used was derived from animals' intestines. The experiment was not a success. In 1734 a new system of street lighting was introduced which dispelled some of the nocturnal gloom. To contemporaries, especially provincials, it was a spectacular achievement. But it remained practically the only one of the period. Gay's *Trivia* and Johnson's *London*, as well as the accounts of travellers, English and foreign, show London to have been squalid and pestiferous, lacking the common amenities; a city of violent contrasts between luxury and elegance and poverty and ugliness. A city, above all, of crime and turbulence and hard living.

At the head of urban society were the merchant princes, with whom a few lawyers and high civil servants could associate on terms of equality both in wealth and social standing. Towards the end of their careers, these merchants often bought up great estates to endow themselves with the social prestige which went with land ownership and which would enable their sons and daughters to marry into the aristocracy or to acquire a title in their own right. These were the men who controlled the Bank of England and the great chartered companies and jealously protected their privileges. They had close financial ties with the government and it is not surprising that in politics they tended to support Walpole and call themselves Whigs; but of course to them Whiggery was not a radical creed. It meant, quite simply, the Hanoverian dynasty, with toleration to dissenters and the preservation of things as they were. In habits of life, the merchant princes differed little from the noblemen; they lived in equal state, built as grandly, and spent as prodigiously on furniture, food, and servants. But not all merchants were merchant princes. The great majority were middling people, mildly prosperous because of their industry and thrift which bred a distinctive ethos. Among these, the ordinary merchants and prosperous shopkeepers, the traditions of seventeenth-century life were stronger. They were still deeply attached to the puritan attitude; many were dissenters. They were also Whig, but it was an old-fashioned type of Whiggery which did not always see eye to eye with Walpole, for they believed in plain, fair, and honest dealing, and the control of government by a Parliament – not the reverse, which was Walpole's way. They both envied and distrusted the great chartered companies and felt increasingly that they were a hindrance to trade. What loyalty they had to Walpole was strained by the opposition's frequent exposure of corruption in high places. Their natural suspicion was aroused by the talk of England's interests being sacrificed to Hanover. They were devoted readers of *The Craftsman*, the vigorous opposition newspaper, which played on their prejudices; some were taken in and voted Tory, most of them kept to the politics of their fathers. Their fervid isolationism and thirst for empire awaited the voice of Chatham, for the gulf between their world and Bolingbroke's – who attempted to turn them into Tories – was too great to be bridged.

The craftsmen and artisans – the journeymen and apprentices of the great livery companies of London – were the bridge between the rich and the poor. They worked long hours – fourteen was common – for a modest wage which, with the additions made by their wives and children, raised them well above the subsistence level, so long as trade was good. But trade was fickle and the chance of hunger and poverty threaded their lives with anxiety. Also, the changes in industrial organization – the decay of the guild, the spread of a free labour market, the introduction of labour-saving machinery – increased the feeling that they were being dispossessed. Until 1725 they still enjoyed a measure of political power in London, but this was diminished by Walpole, who disliked the spread of opposition views, both Tory and Radical, among them. He disliked even more their tendency to combine in order to insist on their rights under Tudor industrial legislation. It is true that Parliament believed that the artisan had a right to a fixed minimum wage and this it tried to uphold, but it condemned outright combination in the two Acts of 1720 and 1744. Of course, combination went on; industries were small, often very localized, especially in London, and the journeymen met together in their friendly societies and taverns. Among them were many who were literate, and the violent press attacks on the government in *The Craftsman* or *Fog's Weekly* – the rabid Jacobite paper – first stimulated, and then focused, their sense of grievance with life. But again, the cheap food and good years of trade assuaged their animosity and kept it in bounds. The periods of most widespread public hostility to Walpole's government coincide with bad harvests or depressed trade. Nevertheless, the instability of their political opinions in a world without organized public order was a factor to be reckoned with, especially so as they still possessed importance in London politics. By their votes, they confronted Walpole with a hostile Lord Mayor at the most critical moment of his life – the Excise crisis of 1733.

Below the artisans and journeymen were the mass of London's population, the hordes of labourers whose livelihood depended almost entirely on casual employment and who were liable to be dismissed at will. Their lives were a chequered pattern of modest affluence and abject poverty. Their hard, lean faces and shrunken bodies gave a sense of bitter despair to many of Hogarth's prints of London life. Among them, philanthropists such as Coram and Oglethorpe laboured to save the children from crime and whoredom. Their plight stirred the heart of all benevolent men and towards them the mission of Wesley and his disciples was directed. But to the politician they were a nightmare. To the desperate poor, a riot was a clarion call to their instinct to survive, for in the burning and looting there was many a windfall. It mattered little to them what the riot was about and unscrupulous politicians never had difficulty in rousing the mob. Of course, the real poor had no political rights and as yet no one conceived that they should have them, though by the opposition they were used as a threat, and by the government as an excuse for executive action that smacked of tyranny; but all parties were unanimous in feeling that the unbridled licence of the destitute justified the savage intensification of the laws dealing with crimes against property, so that, by 1740, for stealing a handkerchief worth one shilling, so long as it was removed privily from the person, children could be hanged by the neck until dead.

*

The big provincial towns were like London but with less wealth and more poverty, more despair, less social order, less charity, more disease, but, like London, full of opportunity for men of tough temperament, endless vigour, and resource to acquire the modest affluence necessary to enter the demi-paradise of comfort and ease which the eighteenth century afforded for hard cash. With property came standing in society and a future for one's children, for in the early part of the century it was relatively easy to pass from one social class to another – a fact which amazed Voltaire and others.

*

This was truer of the great towns than of rural England. Here the pattern of life was more stable, controlled firmly by tradition and custom. Changes there were, such as, in the thirties, the introduction of the turnip and four-fold rotation of crops by Lord Townshend and the development of seed drilling and horse hoeing by Jethro Tull, but they were completely unnoticed by the bulk of the farmers, whether gentlemen or peasant. They farmed as their for-bears had farmed for centuries. The wasteful open-field strip system, only slowly giving way before enclosure, still dominated English agriculture.* Breeding was unselective and the majority of commons and pastures were over-stocked with lean sheep and undernourished cattle. Inefficient as the farming was, the profits were very great. There was an incessant demand for wool and the government bounty on corn stimulated arable farming. The big farming profits encouraged the movement towards enclosure. It also made the possession of great estates a highly desirable form of investment and of course this again encouraged experiments in agrarian technique.

From the end of the seventeenth century, possibly since the Civil War, there had been a tendency for estates to grow larger, and this was beginning, by the early eighteenth century, to affect the nature of rural society. By prudent marriages and careful purchases, some of the aristocratic families of the seventeenth century amassed estates which made them far richer than many of the sovereign powers of Germany. The Duke of Newcastle in 1714 possessed estates in twelve different counties and his income was £40,000 p.a. The Dukes of Bedford were richer; scarcely an acre of Bedfordshire did not belong to them: in every county there were a few families, usually aristocratic, who possessed similar riches. This made them a class apart from the small squire. The distinction was further underlined by the way of life which these agrarian millionaires designed for themselves. The point of pride was the rural palace. There was no modesty felt about the ostentation of wealth. Castle Howard, Wentworth Woodhouse, Houghton intoxicated contemporaries with their size and grandeur. To give them a fit setting nature was subdued with exquisite art and the English

*Enclosure was the replacement of two or three large open fields round a village, whose strips were owned individually but whose crops and stock were controlled by the community of owners, according to ancient rights and practices, by smaller, individually owned fields whose cropping and stocking could be controlled by the owner. Such a change affected the whole structure of rural society.

countryside enriched eternally by men so confident of themselves that they designed for their children's children. Europe first, and Asia next, were ransacked for treasures, modern or antique, good, bad, or indifferent: so long as they emanated a sense of *luxe* they were welcome. Trees, plants, and fruits which have been thoroughly assimilated into the English garden or countryside were then new and strange. The Duke of Argyle introduced the weeping willow and acacia: fuchsia appeared in 1732.

The lesser gentry were in a dilemma. It was difficult for them to suppress either their envy or their desire to emulate their betters. Their envy was further quickened because the possession of vast estates carried greater significance than the ownership of land. For with this ownership went a host of social and political privileges which drew to their possessors the anxious and devoted attention of all aspiring men. As the social and political power of the magnates grew, that of the lesser gentry diminished. Those who had once been courted were now ignored. Naturally, they began to look back to a world of the past in which they believed they had possessed undisputed control of their countryside. So men whose fathers had voted for Shaftesbury or welcomed William III as a deliverer turned Tory. What strength and vigour the Tory party possessed in the early part of the century sprang from the social animosity of the country gentlemen of modest means, but the general prosperity which they shared with all classes took away some of the bitterness which a class, losing power, must feel.

There were a few winners and a multitude of losers lower in the social scale of rural society, although both were fewer than later in the century. The agricultural labourer had eked out a precarious living by using his small allotments and his common rights, but with enclosure, which always required a considerable capital expenditure, these disappeared, and the consequence was a growth in rural poverty which became the nightmare of local administration. The small proprietor – the peasant or yeoman – suffered in a similar way. More often than not he lacked the capital for enclosure: if he was a small tenant farmer, he became unprofitable to his landlord and out he went. The dispossessed swelled the ranks of the rural poor or were eaten up by the towns. Yet not all the yeomen suffered. The landlords wanted intelligent and industrious men to work the new large farms and these the yeomen class provided, but for one who prospered there were a score who lost.

Hungry men will snare and poach. For decades country gentlemen, great or small, had been paying increasing attention to their property rights over the birds of the air or the fish in the streams. As they controlled Parliament, it was easy to give the force of law to their desires; and the poor went hungrier than before. Nevertheless, they were not allowed to die of starvation. The Elizabethan poor law, later modified by the Stuarts, was still operative. The parish was responsible for relief. In the twenties and thirties of this century the problem of the rural poor, especially in South England, became too heavy for the single parish to bear. In 1723 Parliament enabled parishes to combine for the purpose of erecting a workhouse – hence the word 'Union' which is often still applied by the poor to workhouses. These 'unions' were then hired out to any manufacturer who, in return for keeping the inmates alive, obtained cheap labour. To prevent the pauper children absconding they were at times ringed by the neck or manacled. In lean years the despair of the poor became unendurable; food riots, with burning, looting, and mob violence were a commonplace. The militia suppressed them and hangings and transportations followed. Rural poverty and the fear of workhouses does much to explain the lure of the disease-ridden and dangerous life of the towns.

CHAPTER TWO

TRADE AND WEALTH

1714–42

UPON the whole, to sum it up in a few words [wrote Daniel Defoe in 1728] Trade is the Wealth of the World; Trade makes the Difference as to Rich and Poor, between one Nation and another; Trade nourishes Industry, Industry begets Trade; Trade dispenses the natural Wealth of the World, and Trade raises new Species of Wealth, which Nature knew nothing of; Trade has two Daughters, whose fruitful Progeny in Arts may be said to employ Mankind; namely

MANUFACTURE

and

NAVIGATION

Trade was a national preoccupation and the constant concern of Parliament and the government, for all his contemporaries were agreed with Defoe that trade was the cause of England's increasing wealth. The trade of England, both overseas and domestic, was extremely rich and varied, based partly on things made or grown at home and partly on an extensive re-export trade of raw materials from the colonies in America and luxury goods from the East. In order to encourage trade, Walpole removed all restrictive measures on the export of English manufactured goods. He also allowed into the country the raw materials needed for them duty free. But, of course, there was no general tendency towards free trade. Everyone, including Walpole, believed that English manufacturers had to be protected at all costs. The Irish were forbidden to make cloth or export their wool to anywhere but England in case the greatest of all English industries – cloth manufacture – should be endangered in any way. This fear of foreign competition was at times carried to fantastic lengths: it was an offence to shear sheep within four miles of the coast in case the fleeces should be smuggled overseas. Yet this attitude – absurd as it might be in many manifestations – was fundamentally realistic. Eighteenth-century politicians realized with great clarity that wealth meant power. Chatham, who was more preoccupied with England's grandeur than any other statesman, planned his campaigns with the merchants of London and planned them to capture French trade. For trade was wealth and wealth was power.

This was true, too, of the men engaged in commerce and industry; it was the middlemen, the clothiers in the cloth trade, the hostmen in coal, the men who controlled the buying and selling, who had become the dominating figures in English industry in the early part of the century. They gave active encouragement to new processes and often found the money for them. By their demand for more and more goods, craftsmen were forced to consider the efficiency of their industrial processes and look for methods by which output could be increased. One method was by the division of labour so that one workman specialized in one simple process and so produced more; another was the replacement of a workman by a machine which was usually quicker and more accurate; a third was to simplify the product and spend less time, money, and energy in embellishment and decoration. All of these developments can be traced in English clockmaking in the early decades of the eighteenth century; and from being a highly specialized craft in the hands of a few master craftsmen, clockmaking became a widespread national industry whose products by their efficiency and cheapness captured the European market.* It was because division of labour had already proved itself so efficacious,

*Cf. R. W. Symonds, *A History of English Clocks*, King Penguin, 1947.

especially in the metal trades, that Adam Smith championed it so vigorously in his *Inquiry into the Wealth of Nations*.

Division of labour could accomplish a great deal, but there was a limit to what it could do, and in some industries, especially textiles, little further help was to be expected; the only hope for a future increase in output lay in improved technology. In the textile trades there was always a shortage of yarn, for spinning had to be done by hand and output failed to keep pace with weaving or knitting. To overcome the shortage, Irish yarn was imported, but this could be only a stop-gap. The solution was a spinning machine, and several inventors tried to solve this problem: in the thirties a factory with such a machine was started at Northampton, but it was not a success. But it is important to remember that an active search for technological improvement had started long before Arkwright and Hargreaves produced their inventions. In the other two great English industries – coal and iron – there was an equal need for technological improvement.

The demand for coal was so great in the early eighteenth century that it is almost possible to speak of a coal rush. Gentlemen prospected for it on their estates and when, like Lord Paget, they found it under their flower beds, lawns, and parkland, they uprooted the lot without compunction. New finds were not sufficient to meet the demands or to replace the exhaustion of the rich surface, or near surface, seams. The answer was to go deeper, but depth meant flooding. However, the steam pump of Savery and Newcomen, perfected in 1712, solved this problem and secured the most important of England's basic industries. Had they not done so, one of the most important discoveries of the early years of the century would have been almost useless.

After cloth and coal, the most vital of English industries was the metal trade. Iron was smelted by charcoal, but English forests were being rapidly exhausted and in Queen Anne's time it seemed as if the iron industry, and the metal trades which depended on it, were doomed. The experts knew that smelting by coal was the answer and for half a century they tried to discover how to do it. The solution was found by the Darbys of Coalbrookdale, who were using coke for smelting by 1713, and their process was perfected by the thirties. Yet no knowledge of this invention spread for many years because the Darbys realized that firms could be protectionist as well as nations, and with a similar profit. Without this invention and its wide diffusion, England would not have led the world in the industrial revolution which was based on the marriage between coal and iron. These England had in royal abundance; but their rapid exploitation in the middle years of the century was due to these early discoveries.

Jealous of her own inventions and the supremacy of her industries, England viewed those of other nations with an envious eye. Naturally she welcomed Protestant refugees from France, especially when they brought the secret of new industrial processes, but the most spectacular achievement in this field was by the brothers Lombe, an achievement which caught the nation's imagination. In Italy, the manufacture of silk yarn was highly mechanized, though its mechanization was a profound secret; but, in 1716, John Lombe went to Italy and managed to steal plans of the machines which he and his brother, Thomas, patented on his return. A vast factory, 400 feet long, which became one of the sights of England, was built on an island at Derby. Unfortunately John died but, in fifteen years, Thomas had made a fortune of £120,000 and earned a knighthood. In 1732, the patent lapsed, but a grateful Parliament bestowed £14,000 on Thomas and the industry, now open to all, spread rapidly. The success of Lombe fascinated men of the time because it was a successful experiment in the new industrial technique – machines and factories.

English industrialists and merchants were aggressive, inventive, and fully alive to a sense of their own future and greatness. They had the active and intelligent sympathy of the government and yet, compared with the development later in this century or in the early nineteenth, progress was painfully slow. Why was this?

Firstly, the organization of many industries and much of the overseas trade cramped rather than aided their development. Foreign trade was dominated by the great chartered companies – East India, South Seas, African, and Levant – whose directors were the merchant princes of England. The names of these companies indicate the foreign lands of whose trade they enjoyed the monopoly. To many smaller merchants such a restrictive policy was irksome, and the territories of all these companies were invaded by energetic, free-trading interlopers, but the Companies repressed them at every opportunity. The directors of these great companies were also very frequently directors of the Bank of England and, in consequence, their financial relationship with the government was very close, and this helped them to secure their monopolies. It also turned them into sound Walpolean Whigs, in the interests of trade averse to war, which might endanger their magnificent and secure profits.

Industry, too, suffered from the nature of its organization. Conventionally, the organization of industry was still that laid down by Tudor legislation, with its guilds composed of masters, journeymen, and apprentices, and its careful regulations and detailed specifications in regard to the product. Many men, especially those not actively engaged in business, still felt that it was the right method of industrial organization; so did the skilled workmen whose livelihood was endangered by the decay of guild control. The Statute Book is full of Acts attempting to prevent this decay and in the textile industry combinations of workmen were formed in an attempt to secure their rights, and, at Tiverton, they were so desperate that they used firearms. It was the constant industrial unrest, caused by the attitude of masters and middlemen, that led Walpole to make laws against combination and to make it a capital offence to break machinery.

But probably a far greater hindrance to rapid commercial and industrial expansion was the lack of capital and the appalling state of the country's transport system.

The financial panic of the South Sea Bubble led the government to pass the Bubble Act of 1721, which forbade the formation of joint-stock companies without a royal charter – an instrument which was costly and difficult to get; and, therefore, the easiest method of raising the capital necessary for large-scale industrial organization was not available. Further, investors were attracted by the government funds which provided an extremely sound investment with an adequate return. In consequence, many of the new industrial undertakings – such as that of the Darbys of Coalbrookdale – were painstakingly built up by their craftsmen founders, and such a process was long, laborious, and fraught with danger. The position was made worse by a scarcity of banks in the provinces, and so the enterprising industrialists were denied the financial facilities so necessary for the growth of their business.

A more serious obstacle, and one fully appreciated by contemporaries, was the state of transport. The roads were repaired by the inhabitants of the parish through which they passed, which meant that they were never repaired until they were in a desperate condition, and the eighteenth century's idea of a desperate condition was extremely generous – men and horses were drowned in the pot-holes of the Great North Road. For most of the year the roads were a wilderness of bog and swamp and at all times they were infested with swarms of armed robbers – the highwaymen who, like the gangsters of America, captured popular imagination, but were the despair of the travelling merchants. On roads such as these pack horses were the only method of moving goods for any distance and pack horses were a very expensive method. But on the great rivers of England and along the coast water-borne trade moved easily, freely, quickly, and cheaply. And so the early eighteenth century saw an intensified effort to bring more and more of the heart of England in the reach of its water-borne trade. Rivers were deepened and canalized and the flow of water was controlled by locks and sluices. By these means trade with Derby, Nottingham, Bedford, Leeds, Wakefield, Halifax, Wigan, Manchester, and scores of other inland towns became water-borne in the early years of the century. The goods which they produced were cheapened and they reached a national instead of a local market. There were regions which were inaccessible and enterprising men obtained private acts of Parliament by which they were empowered to take over the maintenance of a section of a road and in return allowed to charge a fee for its use. These bodies were called Turnpike Trusts, but in the early part of the century they did very little to help road transport. The trustees were interested in fees more than in repairs. It was only about London, where the trustees were personally interested in the ease of transport, that real improvements were made.

The appetite of England had been whetted by the rapid commercial expansion. A world of never-ending luxury could be won by vigorous and aggressive action against her competitors; so it seemed to many of London's merchants. That war would bring commercial wealth was a deep-seated belief which influenced English politics profoundly. But there were some who believed that England's greatness lay in invention, in discipline, in method, in cheap mass production. To these the relics of a past social order were burdensome and oppressive, but, as yet, only in economic life was it the dawn of their world. In the structure of society their place was modest and obscure.

CHAPTER THREE

SCIENCE AND CULTURE OF THE AUGUSTAN AGE

THE changes in technology, the discovery of new markets in strange lands, the introduction of new plants and fruits were the result not of accident but of design. Englishmen were great travellers in the eighteenth century, but they travelled with a purpose, never purely for pleasure. The aristocrat on his Grand Tour studied languages, politics, constitutions, collected for his palace and his garden; but from their letters it is surprising how many kept open a weather eye for improvements in agricultural technique, for crafts and manufactures which England lacked and for markets which her merchants might exploit. At home, there was a similar search for improvement. The developments in science in the seventeenth century had opened immense vistas in knowledge, deepened man's understanding, and made him question the whole nature of that biblical universe in which his ancestors had believed with unquestioning faith. The Englishman's horizon, both geographical and intellectual, was expanding with great rapidity, and curiosity grew with what it fed upon.

Undoubtedly the first great creative period of English science was over by 1714. Sir Isaac Newton remained President of the Royal Society until his death in 1727, but his work belonged to the past. His ideas and methods dominated the study of the physical and mathematical sciences, but his famous controversy with Leibniz over the differential calculus made his followers obstinately adhere to Newtonian notation. This impeded progress in mathematics. Apart from the Reverend Stephen Hales, who published in 1727 his *Vegetable Staticks*, in which considerable and fundamental contributions were made to chemistry and botany, there were few scientists of importance, although there were many at school absorbing the new knowledge. The age of Walpole was rather an age of diffusion and assimilation in which man's attitude to the universe was readjusted.

Men are loath to wait on observation and experiment before they attempt to explain the nature of the physical world, and it seems equally impossible for them to accept it unexplained. The triumphs of reason had been too startling in the seventeenth century for intelligent men to accept unquestioned the dogmatic theology of an earlier age. The great problem for philosophers and theologians of the early eighteenth century, as it has been ever since science began to dominate intellectual life, was to reconcile reason with religion. The preacher and the publicist did this easily enough by playing down miracles, banishing the terrors of hell, mocking fervour, and stressing the reasonable nature of Christian ethics. God was depersonalized and became the *primum mobile*; whilst deism avoided the dark and irrational problems of evil and guilt. Pope and Bolingbroke were the fashionable exponents of deism, supported by a multitude of theological writers, clerical and lay. Naturally, others sprang to the defence of the older attitudes to Christianity and the twenties and thirties witness a violent theological controversy. The interest in this battle of books was not confined to the participants, for religious literature was easily, then as now, the best seller. It is not difficult to understand why. The views put forward by Toland, Clarke, and Benson were as revolutionary and as startling as those of Huxley and Darwin in a later age. Philosophy was affected by the same sceptical spirit which achieved its clearest expression in David Hume's *Treatise on Human Nature* (1738), but philosophy, unlike theology, had a poor market and the

only favourable review which the book received was a eulo-
gistic notice published by the author himself.

The terrestrial globe needed the light of reason as much as
the nature of the physical universe or the mysteries of God.
Since Hakluyt and Purchas, travel literature had grown
more popular and, with the spread of England's commercial
interests, the demand increased. In the twenties and thirties
the output of travel books was second only to theology, and
Defoe's *Crusoe* and Swift's *Gulliver* were narrations of a very
common theme. Most of the travel books had a more serious
purpose than entertainment. They contained descriptions
of new countries, of their trading prospects and the navigation required by their coasts. Most of them were sold at the
docks and found their way into mariners' chests, for the seas
of the world were still largely uncharted and unmapped.
The principal difficulty was the impossibility of ascertaining
the correct longitude and, in 1714, a Board of Longitude
had been set up and £20,000 offered for the solution of the
problem, which was not arrived at until the age of Chatham,
when John Harrison perfected a chronometer, successfully
used by James Cook.

*

Every political or religious development produced a plethora
of pamphlets: newspapers multiplied in the provinces as well
as in London. A very shrewd Swiss traveller, de Saussure,
wrote in 1727, 'All Englishmen are great newsmongers.
Workmen habitually begin the day by going to coffee rooms
in order to read the daily news. Nothing is more entertaining
than hearing men of this class discussing politics and topics
of interest concerning royalty.' The demand for news was
not confined to London. When George I came to the throne
there were only eight provincial newspapers, all started
since 1700, but, when he died in 1727, seventeen more had
been successfully established.

The widespread demand for books, pamphlets, and newspapers was due to a very considerable growth in literacy. Since the Revolution the number of undergraduates at the universities was rapidly declining. The reasons for this are obscure and a matter for argument. Although higher education decayed, primary education improved immensely through the charity school movement. This began in the latter years of the seventeenth century. At first, the schools were run largely by Dissenters, and then by mixed bodies of Anglicans and Dissenters, who were also associated together in the three other societies concerned with moral education – the Society for Propagation of Christian Knowledge, the Society for the Propagation of the Gospel in Foreign Parts, and the Society for the Reformation of Manners. However, by the reign of George I the charity school movement was dominated by High Anglicans and Tories, some said by Jacobites. It provided education for the artisans' and small shopkeepers' children. In the expanding world of commerce there was an ever-increasing demand for clerks, and these schools provided them. Whatever the politics, the attitude of the men and women who ran these societies was essentially puritan. They believed, like their grandparents before them, in godliness, industry, and thrift. They were very ready to impose their intolerant attitude on a world which was reckless, dissolute, and orgiastic. In 1735, for example, there were 99,380 actions taken out by the Society for the Reformation of Manners in the London area alone. It was, of course, from these people that the leaders of Methodism were to be recruited.

The products of the charity schools and the newly-founded grammar schools made the profession of letters, if rarely self-supporting, at least profitable as a side-line, and there was a great increase in literature other than theology and travel. Vast quantities of poetry and plays, good, bad, and indifferent, were produced, but as yet novels were comparatively rare. The last years of Walpole's ministry saw the beginning of a new phase in fiction with the publication of Samuel Richardson's *Pamela* in 1740. Much the best work of the Augustan age was in satire. The fashionable world of letters was small and intimate, yet large enough to allow social and political feuds to arise which provided material for men such as Pope and Swift, who combined supreme literary gifts with a rich, natural malice. Others unwisely attempted to follow; they are pilloried in the *Dunciad*. The wise and the cautious, like Young and Thomson, wrote smooth, elegant, formal verse to gratify the conventional tastes of their patrons. The growth of literature and the development of journalism deeply affected the writing of prose. The ornate embellishment of seventeenth-century writing, with its effective, deeply personal use of words, disappeared. It is replaced by plainer writing and a simpler vocabulary within the range of the simply educated.

In the eighteenth century London and the provincial towns were faced with a housing shortage unequalled until modern times. And so, in a world of desperate overcrowding, men of all classes were eager to escape to the local pub, and enjoy the undisturbed company of their friends. Some, like Johnson's 'Club', added to our cultural heritage: others, like the apprentices' Cock and Hen clubs, were squalid breeding grounds of crime; the most socially valuable were the friendly (clubs and) societies whose members were bound together, not only for conviviality but also for mutual charity, which, in the dark uncertainties of eighteenth-century life, was ever in demand. But they all made for quick interchange of opinion among men of the same class and tastes, for quick, active discussion of personalities and policies which touched their lives, and so helped to foster that sense of independence and decisive judgement which made England capable of democracy long before the reform of her oligarchic institutions.

The age of Walpole was rough, coarse, brutal; a world for the muscular and the aggressive and the cunning. The thin veneer of elegance and classic form obscured but never hid either the crime and dissipation or the drab middle-class virtue and thrift. For the majority of England, life was hard and vile, but the expanding world of commerce and the rich harvests brought both prosperity and opportunity, which bred a boundless self-confidence. As buildings were torn down to make way for new, ancient barrows became grottoes and Burlington and Kent never doubted for a moment that their buildings and gardens were finer and in better taste than all that had gone before.

I do not think [wrote de Saussure in 1727, and he was not the only visitor to stress the point] there is a people more prejudiced in its own favour than the British people, and they allow this to appear in their talk and manners. They look on foreigners in general with contempt, and think nothing is as well done elsewhere as in their own country.

They needed all their confidence to see them through a century of war in which they lost one empire and gained another. What is more, only a prosperous and self-confident people could have accepted, critically perhaps but with much tolerance, the fantastic hybrid of medieval and Tudor institutions by which their lives were governed.

CHAPTER FOUR

LOCAL GOVERNMENT AND POLITICS

THERE was one factor of great importance about life both in the town and in the countryside. It arose from the smallness of the population. This meant that it was much easier for those who exercised political power or were born to privilege to know one another quite intimately. For instance, in 1726, there were only 179 English peers; some of these were old, some minors, and some witless, so that the active body of the peerage was only about 130, which meant that they knew all about one another, their families, their estates, their habits, views, and political tendencies. Similarly, in the counties, the number of people who really mattered were familiars if not friends, and the same was true of towns. An active politician was able to know his world with a wealth of detail which would be impossible now. The result was to make politics more personal, intimate, and clannish, and, as we shall see, the institutions of government were very appropriate to such a world.

The basic unit of government in England in 1714 was, as it had been in Elizabeth's day, the parish, in which the inhabitants elected their own unpaid officials – the churchwardens, the overseers of the poor, the surveyors of highways, the constables. These were under the immediate supervision and control of the Justice of the Peace, who in rural England was the squire: in the corporate towns, the alderman: and, in the industrial suburbs of London, a rogue who bought his office and traded justice. In the early years of the century Justices, outside the Home Counties, were infrequent, and usually squires of modest means, but, as the

century progressed, their ranks were swelled by the clergy-
men whose social status was rising as they became men of
leisure and ceased to be peasant farmers. The administrative and judicial powers wielded by the Justice were exceptionally large, for, as the parish proved itself incompetent
or unwilling to administer itself, the burden was shifted to
the Justice's shoulders. The entire life of the countryside
came under his control. The simpler forms of justice and
administration he could dispense in his own parlour. With
one brother Justice, sitting in what was called Petty Sessions,
he could deal with another very considerable range of business. Weightier affairs were dealt with four times a year at
Quarter Sessions, when all the Justices of the county met
together. Naturally, Quarter Sessions provided an admirable opportunity to discuss national as well as local politics,
and, of course, to decide on parliamentary candidates. In
time, one of the Quarter Sessions became more important
than the rest, and to this all the leading county dignitaries
would come. From time to time, this body would take
decisions of fundamental importance to English social life,
and to these decisions they themselves gave the force of law.
For example, the famous 'Speenhamland Act' of 1795,
which altered fundamentally English poor relief by making
the parish responsible for making up the labourer's wage to
subsistence level, was merely the decision of one of these
local legislatures, in this case the Berkshire magistrates. As
Justices they enforced it and other Justices followed suit.
This indicates something of the Justices' power. Naturally,
some were tempted to abuse it, and the caricatures of rural
tyrants in Fielding and Smollett had their counterparts in
real life. There were others such as Sir Onesiphorus Paul
or the Reverend Richard Burn who devoted their lives to
the attempt to make local administration and justice more
efficient and less corrupt. Towards the end of the century,
men such as these began to insist that the county should

employ paid officials – such as a Treasurer or a Surveyor –
so that business would be carried out speedily and effectively, and it was on these modest foundations that the great
fabric of nineteenth-century local administration was built.*

Above the Justice were a number of county officials such
as Sheriff, Deputy Lieutenant, Lord Lieutenant, whose
administrative functions had largely disappeared, but they
were still officers of considerable social and political importance. The Lord Lieutenant was of exceptional political
importance because he was usually a peer of ministerial
rank or high court official and, as such, was the principal
local vehicle of crown patronage, the biggest wire that could
be pulled. The Duke of Newcastle, the century's greatest
exponent of the art of patronage, kept for himself the Lord
Lieutenancy of the three counties where his estates were
largest and his need of influence was greatest. The Lord
Lieutenant also controlled the appointment of Justices of
the Peace.

The government of towns was more complex. The nature
of their constitution had nothing whatsoever to do with
their size or importance. Haverfordwest, a fishing hamlet in
Pembrokeshire, had the same rights and privileges as the
City of London. Manchester and Birmingham were not
towns, only parishes, and they had the same constitution as
a village, and in consequence they were ignorant of the
blessings of organized administration or justice. The old-
established county towns such as Norwich, Bristol, Lincoln,
or Leicester had a certain similarity. They were chartered
corporations, which meant that many of their powers,
though not all, were defined by royal charter. In the past,
they had had a mildly democratic character, but by the
eighteenth century almost all of them were dominated by
families of self-perpetuating oligarchs, utterly uninterested
in social administration, who squandered and abused

*Cf. also pp. 86–7.

corporate wealth and corporate charities. No matter how obscurantist, incompetent, or corrupt they proved themselves to be, no government in the eighteenth century attempted to modify their powers or limit their privileges, for it was such an attempt which had contributed so much to the final downfall of James and the success of the Revolution of 1689. To local oligarchs, urban or rural, Whig or Tory, the Revolution of 1689 was sacrosanct.

*

One of the major preoccupations of the Justices of the Peace and of the aldermen and burgesses, as well as of the aristocracy, the landed gentry, and even the clergy, was the endless political intrigue and patronage hunting which was associated with elections to the House of Commons. The Unreformed House of Commons consisted of 513 members for England and Wales and 45 for Scotland. Each English county returned two members and every freeholder with 40 shillings p.a. was allowed to vote in their election. But of course, freeholders were usually tenants as well, and as voting was open – the squires scrutinized the poll books to make certain that their tenants voted according to their dictation – most tenants obeyed their masters. The result was that county elections became struggles between rival clans and families in which the animosity of the less wealthy was, at times, concentrated against the great. Sometimes, in order to avoid the vast expense of an election – for tenants had to be transported to the polling booth and entertained with beef and beer – a compromise solution was made by which one member was returned by the Whig aristocracy and the other by the Tory gentry, but personal feuds could always shatter such arrangements or the violence of a political crisis lure one party into attempting to capture both seats. A battle of giants would follow and, for a large county, expenses might reach £100,000 or even more.

The number of votes a peer or squire could secure either by threats, promises, or bribes was the measure of his influence; and a man in eighteenth-century politics was assessed by his influence. If it were large, he could trade it for very concrete profits – places and pensions and jobs for his relatives and dependants, and, the more of these he could secure, the more lesser men of influence he attracted to his constellation of power, which enabled him in turn to increase his demands and weight his threats against a ministry reluctant to gratify him. In a world where there were no appointments by examination or interviewing boards, where every office was in the gift of someone else, it is obvious that an extremely complex system of political bargaining and blackmail must arise. This is true of the eighteenth century and it permeates all the institutions of government. The control of parliamentary votes was the basic coin of this traffic. The counties offered some scope, but it was nothing compared to what the parliamentary boroughs could offer.

The right to return members to Parliament bore no relation to the distribution of population or the size of the town. The majority of towns and villages which had this right were in the south and south-west; one quarter of the House of Commons was returned by five counties – Cornwall (44 M.P.s), Devon (26), Dorset (20), Somerset (18), and Wiltshire (34). The total electorate for boroughs was about 85,000 but, of these, 15,000 voters controlled half the seats. The privilege of voting was rarely conferred on the entire population, only twelve boroughs – the most important of which was Westminster – having anything approaching universal male suffrage. But even universal male suffrage was no indication that the election would be either free or uncorrupt. Gatton in Surrey enjoyed this wide franchise but, as at one time it had only six houses and one voter, the proprietors of the manor regarded it as a pocket borough. On the other hand, Bath with an electorate of 32 pursued a

consistently independent line, whereas Bedford, with an electorate of 1,000, obeyed the commands of the Dukes of Bedford with unfailing subservience and was suitably rewarded.
There is no sure generalization in dealing with eighteenth-
century politics; by and large, small electorates were easier
to control than large ones, but the basis of the control was
human nature – its desires, its appetites, its ambitions – and
human nature may always behave in a wilful or unpre-
dictable way. It was the waywardness and cupidity of
human nature which made the work for electioneering
agents and local political bosses. It meant, too, constant
supervision, constant awareness, constant expenditure. The
last was the critical factor. Between 1689 and 1727, election
costs had mounted very rapidly. Parliament and its control
had become the way to power. In 1727, a seat at Harwich
cost the Earl of Egmont £900: in 1689, Samuel Pepys had
spent there only £8 6s 8d on his unsuccessful election.
These were the years in which election contests were very
common even in constituencies with very small electorates,
because local families were locked in a battle to secure
parliamentary influence, sometimes on personal, sometimes
on party grounds. But, owing to the growing expense,
many families were dropping out of the struggle and amal-
gamating their interest with wealthier patrons. The passing
of the Septenniel Bill in 1716 and the rise of the Duke of
Newcastle to power greatly accelerated this process. The
Septennial Bill meant that Parliaments lasted for seven
instead of three years, and that therefore men were prepared
to spend twice as much as before. This benefited the very
wealthy and worked against the electoral interests of the
smaller gentry. The Duke of Newcastle had a passion for
electioneering politics and, after he became Secretary of
State in 1724, he controlled government patronage for
nearly forty years. Before this the government influence
had not been fully exploited, but he made certain that the

meanest government official in the Customs and Excise, or in the service of the Admiralty or the Post Office, had to use his vote, if he had one, in accordance with instructions or lost his job. This meant that in many seaports the government began to exercise a controlling influence which, when combined with the chief local interest, became almost absolute. As the government was the fountain-head of powers, large or small, patrons were ready enough for this alliance. The greatly increased cost of elections quite often made it imperative for them to secure an office of profit under the crown for themselves and their henchmen. New-castle, in 1727, made the relationship more intimate. In return for the right to nominate members, Newcastle began to make direct financial grants from the secret service money. The value of a nomination was assessed at £1,500, a figure which remained fairly constant. Election contests began to disappear; in 1761 there were only fifteen contests in boroughs where the electorate was under 400, whereas in 1715 there had been over sixty. But the broader effect was this. The government machine in alliance with the major borough patrons could be certain of victory at any general election; and so, winning the heart of the electorate became of diminishing importance to eighteenth-century politicians. In opposition, they exerted all their skill to win over patrons of importance, then to provoke a ministerial crisis, and in the resulting intrigues to capture the Treasury, a manoeuvre of great strategic and tactical complexity, frequently attempted and rarely achieved.

For every parliamentary seat, someone's interest was of importance, but, in so complex and yet so intimate a world, interest alone was frequently not enough and wider issues might prevail. In any case, the age did not believe in demo-cracy; the world of authority belonged to owners of property and not to the dispossessed. What protest there was, at least for three quarters of the century, was concerned not with the electoral machine itself but the way it was being worked in favour of the very rich and of government officials. Bills for annual parliaments, bills against bribery, bills for the exclusion of placemen were aimed at Newcastle and his methods and all that he symbolized, not at the nature of Parliament itself. Nevertheless it is doubtful if any member of the ruling class, no matter how odd or eccentric his political views, was ever kept out of Parliament, if he really wanted to get in. For the young, energetic politician, election to the Commons was far easier than in the nineteenth or twentieth centuries. Naturally, patrons were careful to select members whose views would not compromise their relations with the government, and it was considered common courtesy to resign if conscience dictated a vote in conflict with the patron's wishes, but there were always patrons of boroughs in opposition or electorates like Bath which preferred independent and pugnacious men. In consequence, eighteenth-century parliaments always had a leaven of vigorous, enterprising young men, eager to make their name, and this prevented the Commons from becoming moribund and servile.

Political society was, of course, extremely intimate and inbred and this, as well as the intrigue for place and the control of influence, led to the development of clans as well as factions. For a member, like Joseph Ashe in 1710, to have fifty relatives who were M.P.s was a commonplace. At the head of these clans there was usually a peer who aspired and intrigued for ministerial office, and his standing was measured by the number and reliability of the relatives he controlled. Both houses of Parliament contained a number of pressure groups, bound closely by family as well as political ties. Their attempts to secure or retain office clutter the history of the eighteenth century with trivial detail and obscure the deeper issues which were involved.

CHAPTER FIVE

THE PROFESSIONS

On 19 March 1730, the Bishop of Killala in Ireland wrote to his aunt, Mrs Clayton, Mistress of the Robes to Queen Caroline, as follows:

What occurs to me at present is, the considering of ecclesiastical preferments in a political view. It has not been customary for persons of either birth or culture to breed up their children to the Church which means when preferment in the Church is given by their Majesties, there is seldom any one obliged but the very person to whom it is given, having no near relations in the House of Lords or Commons that are gratified or kept in dependence thereby.

The bishop was a little behind the times; a year earlier, George II had declared that he intended to give preferment to all clerics who were gentlemen of quality. There was a pressing necessity, for the demand for place always outran supply. The church had been very little exploited.

The political value of bishoprics was understood. Between 1715 and 1722, the bench was filled with sound Whigs as Anne's Tory bishops died off. Nor did a bishopric bring independence. The minor bishoprics such as St Asaph's, Oxford, or Bristol were worth very little, only £300 p.a., but the aspiring prelate had before him the prospect of rich sees such as Winchester, Durham, or London, worth more than ten times as much. Devotion to the ministry, expressed in constant attendance at the House of Lords, and in the careful management of the diocesan electoral interest, usually secured translation in due time. The slightest flicker of independence in the House of Lords could blight a career. For a speech there, Archbishop Secker was kept for sixteen years in poor sees: only a very long life enabled him to live it down. Bishop Watson remained at Llandaff all his life because he spoke his mind. It meant, of course, that bishops became first and foremost politicians, and politicians are rarely men of the spirit. There is a wordliness, almost a venality, about eighteenth-century prelates which no amount of apologetics can conceal. The clerical duties of visitation, ordination, and confirmation, were done only as political duties allowed. Dioceses were enormous. Lincoln stretched from the Humber to the Thames. There were no suffragans. No bishops retired, so that frequently old age and infirmity created a back-log of gigantic proportions with which the young and energetic tried to cope unavailingly. Most eighteenth-century bishops were not idle but industrious men, who accepted too easily the difficulties which faced them as a part of the unchangeable nature of society.

Below the bishoprics stretched a ladder of preferment; the lowest rung was a village curacy, worth perhaps £30–£40 p.a., the highest was the deanery of a great cathedral which might be worth more than many a bishopric. This was the field which Newcastle began to cultivate with great care after he acquired complete control of clerical patronage in 1736. The value of many of these preferments was rising steadily with the increased exploitation of the nation's wealth; this was true of the ordinary benefice as well as of the prebendaries and deaneries. The clerical life attracted increasingly the younger sons of the nobility or gentry, and to help them collect an income equal to their standing, non-residence was tolerated and plurality encouraged. Contemporaries noticed this change.

'Our grandees,' wrote Bishop Warburton in 1752, 'have at last found their way back into the Church. I only wonder they have been so long about it.' They made up for lost time. By the end of the century, the Duke of Rutland's family, the Manners, had held eight English and twelve Irish sees. In the lower ranks as in the higher, it was the discreet, assiduous politician who was the successful cleric.

The vast majority of parish priests and curates were not quite gentlemen. They were betwixt and between. Many of them farmed their glebe, but the custom grew less common as the century grew older. The agricultural prosperity brought leisure to the parish priests, for their clerical duties were light, communion three times a year and sermons seldom. Time hung heavily on their hands. Some took to drink, some to fox hunting, some to local government, some to learning. The last is important and impressive: Berkeley and Butler in philosophy; Gilbert White in Natural History; Jethro Tull in agriculture; Stephen Hales in chemistry; Sterne in literature; Stukeley in archaeology; Burn in law. They devoted themselves to everything but the administrative reform of the institution to which they belonged. In the north and midlands of England the growth of industrial villages bore no relation to the age-old pattern of parishes, nor did the vast poverty-stricken suburbs of East London. The Church ignored them and Wesley won them for Methodism.

But the greatest danger to the Church lay not only in its refusal to reform but in its attitude to life. The way to success was in discretion and man-pleasing and the worldly virtues became heavenly ones. The most popular sermon in the eighteenth century was Tillotson's on the text: 'His commandments are not grievous', in which he stresses that if a man applies the same principles he uses in business or commerce to his moral life, he will be sure – of what? A *place* in heaven. Evil and guilt, sin and redemption – the whole personal drama and appeal of religion – was forgotten or rationalized away and the eupeptic optimism of politicians pervaded the teaching of the Church. It was not a religion which had much appeal to the men and women living brutal and squalid lives in the disease-ridden slums of the new towns and mining villages. They needed revelation and salvation.

*

Not only bishops earned their bread at Westminster, but generals and admirals, colonels and captains were also made familiar with the rigours of political discipline. The Duke of Bolton and Lord Cobham opposed the ministry in 1733, only to lose their regiments. Once established as a principle, it became a convention, and Ensign Pitt went in 1736 the way of his superiors. At first this aroused great indignation. William Pulteney, a leader of the opposition, called it robbery. He reasoned thus. Commissions had to be bought with cash; therefore, once bought, the owner had a legal title to them as he might have to a piece of land. Many agreed. Commissions were often investments and lucrative ones. Every device was used to make them pay handsome profits. Dead sailors and soldiers were kept on the pay book; the wages of the living were deliberately kept in arrears and their clothing and food were often the worst at the dearest prices. In fact, it was because they were so lucrative that the government's action became so effective. However, the system worked both ways; if misbehaviour meant punishment, good behaviour demanded reward. In 1759 Lord Gage wrote to Newcastle who, of course, controlled military patronage as well as everything else: 'Without entering into a discussion on Mr Townshend's right to a regiment as an officer: I think as a Member of Parliament, his abilities and connexions give him a claim to favour.'

Discretion in politics was the first lesson in strategy that every well-born ensign had to learn; and discretion meant a blind eye to maladministration and incompetence. Fortunately for England, the navy, although riddled by the same sort of political patronage, was never dominated by it, largely because the sailing of ships requires demonstrable skill.

Other professions provided their quota of patronage; in spite of some resistance, the universities were comparatively easy game for Newcastle, especially Cambridge, where he himself secured the Chancellorship. Lawyers were more intractable than dons. Although the highest legal offices were in the gift of the government, the fortunes of practising lawyers in an age prone to protracted litigation were often princely and allowed their owners to indulge themselves in political independence.

CHAPTER SIX

WHITEHALL

So far we have described the outer bulwarks of the constitution, but the citadel was the King's Household, which provided the vast majority of places and sinecures for the loyal. All ministers were the King's servants, appointed by him, dismissed by him, dependent for their powers almost entirely on his prerogative. They were responsible for all of his acts and answerable for them to Parliament as well as to the King; a divided command and one imperfectly understood by both commanders. In fact, the relationship between executive and legislature bewildered contemporary Englishmen as well as foreigners, and it was not only Montesquieu and Voltaire who saw powers separate that were united. Bolingbroke, the chief expositor of constitutional theory in the early decades, felt that the executive had no right to be in Parliament which was to be the judge of its acts, but the practical wisdom of Walpole and Newcastle saw that, if any continuity of policy was to be achieved, the executive needed to be in control. The need was all the more imperative because M.P.s were pledged only to very broad political principles and never to definite political programmes as M.P.s are today. Nor was there any party organization as we know it. Hence, left to its own devices, Parliament would have been an anarchy of individual minds and wills, swayed by the tide of circumstance. The solution to the problem was provided by the King's Household. Government supporters were given places – usually sinecures, such as Master of the King's Tennis Court or Taster of the King's Wines in Dublin – but what is not usually recognized is that many of these offices were filled by men who fulfilled the function of a modern Under-Secretaryship of State or Parliamentary Secretary of a Ministry. The occupants of these sinecure offices were often expected not only to attend debates and vote but also to take an important part in piloting government measures through the Commons. But apart from their parliamentary duties most of the place-holders had nothing to do, and, if they had, then it was usual to appoint a deputy, usually a clerk glad of £50 p.a. Many of them considered that their parliamentary duties were adequately performed if they voted.

Of course, these posts, whether they carried political duties or involved administrative duties about the court, were eagerly sought by members of the aristocracy and their relations. Apart from the very welcome addition of income, the holding of these offices implied social status and political influence, and brought one to the very heart of affairs, foreign or domestic – the Court. The vested interests so created were extremely involved, and even the smallest reform in the administration of the Household might create active displeasure amongst a score of silent voters. Newcastle and Walpole, badgered on all sides by the incessant clamour for place, could not afford to disregard the most archaic or useless office. In the last years of the seventeenth century, there had been a certain reorganization of the Treasury in order to cope with the vast financial transactions demanded by the wars against France and with the increased revenues from customs and excise. But they were the last reforms for nearly a century and the administrative machinery remained a strange mixture of medieval and Tudor. Roman numerals and the Courthand – an almost unreadable script – were still formally used at the Exchequer and so, too, were tallies – willow wands carefully notched and inscribed in Latin and then split down the middle, one half staying with the Exchequer, the other being used as a receipt. Examples of such archaisms could be multiplied. The really vital parts of the machinery, the Treasury and the Secretary of State's department, were grossly understaffed.

The Secretaries of State – there were two – were in charge of all foreign and domestic affairs other than taxation, and they were the principal authority for Scotland, Ireland, the Colonies, and for the Army and Navy. The entire staff – including caretakers – numbered only 24 in 1726. Other departments were in a similar situation and the arrears of business grew steadily; by 1750, accountancy was between 15 and 20 years behind the times. On the other hand, it had advantages; between them the two Secretaries of State and the Chancellor of the Exchequer, who was now also the First Lord of the Treasury, controlled almost the entire life of the nation, which made for the integration of policy.

The great officers of state – including the Archbishop of Canterbury – belonged to the King's Privy Council, but this was now a formal body which had little to do with politics. They also belonged to the Cabinet Council, but this, too, was rapidly going the way of the Privy Council. It was too large a body to discuss either the secret negotiations with foreign powers or the more secret questions of strategy when we were involved in war. Walpole and George II encouraged the development of a small inner cabinet, consisting of the Secretaries, the Lord Chancellor, Lord Privy Seal, Lord President of the Council, and the Chancellor of the Exchequer. This body met informally: it had access to all secret papers and it was here that the real decisions on policy were taken. It was quickly realized that if a minister belonging to this inner circle disagreed with his colleagues on a vital issue he had no alternative but to resign, an attitude which gave rise later to the idea of the collective responsibility of the cabinet. This small inner or efficient cabinet was the true ancestor of the modern cabinet, but still a remote one, and it is extremely misleading to try to impose modern, or nineteenth-century, constitutional ideas on the eighteenth century. This inner cabinet kept few minutes and rarely recorded its decisions, and it met wherever suited best, and often this was at dinner. When its mind was made up the work was not finished, for the minister chiefly concerned would have to secure the consent of the King, and this might mean a great deal of argument, not always attended with success. In this inner ring of ministers there was frequently one who by common consent was the foremost, whose word carried the most weight and who acted as the principal vehicle in their relations with the King. Sometimes he was called the Prime Minister, but usually only by his enemies and as a term of mild abuse. He was still very much the King's servant.

The Court was the heart of political and social life, for all decisions taken, all places promised, from a turnkey to a bishopric, had to be discussed and argued with the King. It is a great fallacy to think that the early Hanoverians were uninterested in English political life. Because they were both stupid and obstinate they were frequently infuriated by the methods and conventions of our constitution, but they realized to the full the immense powers which they possessed. As Walpole wryly remarked: 'Our master, like most people's masters, wishes himself absolute.' On matters within their comprehension, they exercised their powers to the full, and it needed immense pressure to make them change their minds. Fortunately they were crassly stupid, and they could not grasp, as the Stuarts or William III had grasped, the complexities of either foreign or domestic affairs. Both George I and George II, although obstinate, domineering, and excessively prone to interference in detail, were incapable, totally incapable, of forming a policy. Nevertheless, great as the Crown's powers were, Britain was a constitutional monarchy and the only one in the world. The broad issues which this implied were known and accepted. They were these. The King could not be a Roman Catholic. He could not suspend the laws. He depended on Parliament for his income and for his army. His ministers were in the final instance answerable to Parliament and his pardon was no plea to any act which they might have committed. In the final reckoning power was not with him but with Parliament – a position the Hanoverians understood as well as their subjects. But, even so, the Court was the heart of the body politic and the stability of all governments depended on its goodwill, no matter whether with the public at large they were popular or not. Each King had his friends and each King was forced reluctantly to part with them for a time, but never for long.

CHAPTER SEVEN

THE RISE OF SIR ROBERT WALPOLE
1715–22

IN 1714 everyone, even the Tory government, knew that the future belonged to the Whigs. For a long time the Tory leaders had lost contact with the realities of political life and had obstinately refused to face the question of what was to happen on the death of Queen Anne. By the Act of 1705, they knew that the government in power would be dissolved and the Lords Justices, appointed by the Elector of Hanover, the Queen's successor, would take over. The Lords Justices would be Whig, for with unswerving consistency the Whigs had supported the Hanoverian succession, whereas some of the Tories had entertained the idea of bringing back the Stuarts. To bring back the Stuarts meant more than bringing back a Catholic King; it meant power for the conservative forces of society, and an attempt to make the world safe for the squire, parson, and craftsman. That this was the intention of the Tories was clear enough from the Acts which they had recently passed, which had strengthened both the squirearchy and the Church at the expense of merchants and dissenters.

The Tories had further worries. During their period of power, 1710–14, they had shown themselves vindictive to the Whigs – Marlborough's officers had been cashiered from the Army, and Robert Walpole, the most promising of the junior Whig politicians, sent to the Tower on a charge of corruption. If the Whigs came to power, the Tories could expect inquiries into their past conduct and they could be certain that they would be found guilty. Their situation was desperate, calling for bold leadership and quick, firm decisions. It was not forthcoming. There was likewise rivalry between their leaders, Oxford and Bolingbroke; each favoured a different policy. Neither had much support from the other ministers, who were disinclined to take desperate decisions, and willing to face and to accept the inevitable Whig victory. This came quickly with the death of the Queen and the accession of George I, Elector of Hanover, and his arrival in this country. But a Whig victory did not resolve the country's social and political problems.

The country had fought a long war which had created a national debt of over £54,000,000. The annual interest paid on this debt was £3,500,000. These figures dismayed the vast majority of Englishmen. No one had any knowledge of the real wealth of the kingdom and, in consequence, national bankruptcy was regarded as inevitable. War, too, as always, had played havoc with established and customary economic relationships, and readjustment to peacetime economy was haphazard and unplanned. Soldiers had been discharged. Unemployment and poverty came to many craftsmen when the demands for guns, ammunition, and clothing ceased. This was the breeding ground of discontent. Amongst the lower classes there was an almost anarchistic distrust of government and authority, an attitude which Tory propagandists seized on and exploited to their own advantage. Their success was considerable, and Tory and Jacobite mobs were a commonplace in London in the winter of 1714–15. The government was so disquieted that it passed the Riot Act which gave increased power to the Justices of the Peace.

On the other hand their success encouraged the Jacobites to consider direct action. There were other stimulants. By exerting all the resources of influence and patronage, the government and the leading Whig aristocrats had managed to achieve a Whig majority at the general election, which automatically followed the death of the Sovereign. This majority was enough to enable the Whigs to settle down to two tasks; one, the reversal of Tory policy: the second, the punishment and vilification of the Tory leaders and the removal of their underlings from any office, no matter how small, in Church or State, for, as the Whigs well knew, on the thoroughness of the purge would depend the future stability of their party. With a new monarch, all commissions required renewal and most holders of office required confirmation of their right to hold it. So, Tory squires ceased to be J.P.s or Deputy-Lieutenants and, of course, they grumbled and machinated: so did the Tory place-holders, now unemployed. The Tory leaders faced impeachment on the grounds that they had betrayed English interests in the Treaty of Utrecht by which they had concluded the War of the Spanish Succession in 1713. Feeling that their condemnation would be certain, first Bolingbroke, then the Duke of Ormonde, fled the country and joined the Pretender – an act which enabled the Whigs to brand every Tory a Jacobite.

To Bolingbroke and Ormonde there seemed no hope for themselves or for the Tories except by rebellion. The Pretender was eager enough to attempt it, but unwilling to take anyone's advice. In any case the advice was muddled enough. Bolingbroke wanted a landing on the south coast of England and an appeal to the common people. Ormonde advised Scotland and the traditional Jacobite policy – that kingship was divinely ordained to descend according to strict hereditary principles, whether the King was Catholic or Protestant, good or bad. Ormonde wanted to overturn the Revolution of 1689, Bolingbroke to accept it, but Bolingbroke's policy was too novel, too ingenious, to find acceptance in Jacobite circles. In any case, the Earl of Mar settled the argument by leading a rebellion in Scotland in September 1715.

The government was prepared. It had an excellent intelligence service. It agreed with Bolingbroke that the real danger was the south and wisely it kept the bulk of the armed forces about London and sent only a small force under the Duke of Argyle to deal with Mar. Mar required an immediate and decisive victory in order to win all Scotland. His army at Sheriffmuir outnumbered Argyle's by three to one, but Argyle's troops were Marlborough's veterans and they skilfully avoided defeat. It was enough to contain Mar. The rebellion dragged on a few months to its inevitable and disastrous end. The Highlands were ruthlessly harried, leaving bitter memories. Very few of the important Jacobites were caught and very few suffered, a policy dictated as much by the future's uncertain course as by natural clemency. In any case the rebellion had given the Whigs a trump card – Tory and Jacobite had become synonymous. There could be no more thinking in terms of mixed Whig and Tory ministries – it was impracticable politics. The resources of the Crown, the institution of government, and the future all belonged to the Whigs to build their own world. But the Whigs had been in the wilderness for some years and there was no defined leadership of the party. From 1715 to 1721 the major political struggle was between two factions of the Whigs for power, but it was not purely a struggle for power and nothing else. The groups differed on how to make the world safe for Whigs and on how far to undo the work of the last Tory ministry. This was their battle-ground.

The two groups were led by Stanhope and Sunderland on one hand and Walpole and Townshend on the other. Stanhope was a soldier, eager to undo the Treaty of Utrecht, which he considered had humiliated England. He was ready to take up an active and aggressive attitude to any European problem. There were plenty of problems, many left over by Utrecht, others brought over by the King, relating to his German dominions. Stanhope allied England, first with France and the Netherlands (1717), forced the Emperor to join them (Quadruple Alliance, 1718), and used the British

fleet to bring the Spanish to heel in 1718. In Northern
Europe his policy was equally aggressive. Time and time
again he took the risk of war, and knowing it, poured out
subsidies on possible allies and hired mercenaries at a high
cost. His domestic policy had the same warm-hearted, rash
quality. He wanted to sweep away all the restrictive legislation which had been passed since the Restoration of 1660
against the dissenters, and to allow them to enter fully into
English civic life. Although he was willing to remove some
of the intolerable restrictions placed on Roman Catholics,
he had no love for Tories and wanted to reform the Universities of Oxford and Cambridge because he thought they
bred too many of them. There was an impetuosity about
this policy which disturbed many members of Parliament.
They thought that undue risks were being taken at a time
of great social and political difficulty. And behind Stanhope
was the dark, intriguing figure of Sunderland, anxious to
remove all but his own clients and family group from offices
of trust and profit; and Walpole and Townshend could be
sure that even whole-hearted compliance with Stanhope's
policy would not bring them personal security.

But neither Walpole nor Townshend trusted Stanhope's
policy. Some way they could, and did, go with him. They
believed with him that stability must be achieved and the
Whig triumph consolidated, and they supported whole-
heartedly the Septennial Act of 1716, by which general elections were held once in seven instead of once in three years –
an act which doubled the value of influence and patronage
to Whig advantage. Walpole, with Stanhope's support,
tackled the problem of the national debt, and he tackled it
with that human realism of which he was such a master. He
reduced the varied debts with differing interest rates to one
debt bearing a common rate of interest, and he instituted
a Sinking Fund by which each year certain taxes were used
to pay off the debt so that the eventual discharge of the debt

seemed to be within sight. It had a tonic effect. Men and women of the time felt that their money in government loans was secure because it was certain to be repaid.

But, before the Acts necessary to establish the Sinking Fund had been passed, Walpole and Townshend had broken with Stanhope. Walpole was convinced that his financial policy would work only if there was no increase in the national debt. An aggressive foreign policy meant expensive alliances and perhaps an even more expensive war. Time and time again during his career, Walpole insisted on a policy of non-aggression. But, of course, there was more in the split than a difference in policy. Sunderland had the ear of the King's German mistresses; Stanhope was the King's own favourite. The future for both Walpole and Townshend seemed limited and circumscribed. Realizing that there was considerable antipathy to their rivals' policy, they became critical and restive, angling for support in the Commons. Sunderland turned them out of office, and the battle for Whig leadership was on in earnest.

Stanhope went ahead with his policy; the Schism Act and the Occasional Conformity Acts were repealed, but when he attempted to do the same with the Corporation and Test Acts – this would have given the dissenters full civic rights – he met his first defeat. Meanwhile the battle of Passaro (1718) and the dispatch of another fleet to the Baltic hammered home Walpole's repeated warning that Stanhope's policy would lead to war and war to fresh financial disorder. The opposition grew – a curious hybrid mixture of Tories, independently-minded country gentlemen, and Whigs who put their hopes of power and office on Walpole, a pattern for all future eighteenth-century oppositions. It may have disturbed Stanhope, but it certainly did not deter him. The third aspect of Stanhope's policy was to make the world safe for his party and so far, at least on this issue, Walpole had supported him. Now, the Treaty of Utrecht had passed the

House of Lords only because Queen Anne had exercised her prerogative and created twelve Tory peers. If the Crown was deprived of such a right, the Whigs might expect to dominate the House of Lords for a generation, for a whiggish world suited the peerage well enough. Stanhope, therefore, brought forward a Peerage Bill in order to limit the King's prerogative. Walpole denounced the bill as closing the avenue to honour and promotion to which all simple country gentlemen might aspire, if not for themselves, then for their children and their children's children. This argument rallied the back benchers and Stanhope suffered his worst defeat. There was no alternative but to take Walpole and Townshend back into office. They were willing to come in, for opposition was an expensive luxury rather beyond Walpole's pocket. In any case, they wanted power and they had shown how dangerous they could be in opposition; and so they had power to bargain.

No sooner were they back than the government was confronted with a grave political and economic crisis – the South Sea Bubble. Within the last twenty-five years governments had been slowly learning how to handle millions of pounds instead of tens of thousands and, although some knowledge had been gained of the operations of high finance, ignorance was still very great. Sunderland, realizing the impression which Walpole had made by the institution of the Sinking Fund, was willing to consider sympathetically any scheme for liquidating the debt more quickly. The South Sea Company put up a scheme, and backed their suggestion with large grants of shares to leading politicians and the King's mistresses. The Sinking Fund scheme had done much to create confidence and a holiday mood amongst those speculators who had previously expected national bankruptcy; and the South Sea Scheme provoked a wild outburst of speculation which could only lead to financial chaos. The crash came in August 1720. Then the dispossessed

clamoured for victims and revenge. A Parliamentary inquiry was inescapable and both the Court and the Cabinet
were afraid of what would be revealed. Sunderland pushed
Walpole forward, for he was one of the few members of the
Government not involved in the scandal, though more by
luck than judgement. There is no doubt, too, that Sunderland hoped that Walpole's attempt to serve the government
and the Court would destroy Walpole's political capital.

The extrication of the government from the South Sea
scandal is the turning point of Walpole's career. He saved
the Court; he saved what politicians he could; he even
saved something for the South Sea Directors. He ignored
contemptuously the popular hatred he aroused and used all
his parliamentary skill to force through his policy. The
ministry survived: the finances of the country were patched
up: the dynasty had been rescued from overt scandal. The
price for the Stanhope faction had been high. Stanhope
himself died of apoplexy; Sunderland was compelled to
retire. Many of their supporters were disgraced; some died.
In the reconstituted ministry, Walpole became Chancellor of
the Exchequer and First Lord of the Treasury; Townshend,
Secretary of State; and the rest of the vacant offices were
divided equally between the two Whig factions. Although
Walpole had increased his political power enormously,
Sunderland was far from finished, and Walpole made little
further headway until Sunderland suddenly died in 1722.
At last the problem of Whig leadership was resolved. There
was no one of Walpole's stature. Walpole may have lacked
vision; certainly he was not moved by a sense of England's
destiny, but the intimate politics of the eighteenth century
were an involved web of human passions, and Walpole's
shrewd and compassionate understanding enabled him to
dominate men if not circumstance. This deep understanding
of human motive, amounting almost to genius, is the true
foundation of Walpole's greatness.

CHAPTER EIGHT

SIR ROBERT WALPOLE
1722-33

In 1722 Robert Walpole's aims were simple. He wanted stability and prosperity at home; peace abroad; a disgrace, if possible, for the Tories, to eliminate from public memory the distaste of the South Sea scandal; the removal from office of Sunderland's friends, and replacement by his own. Further, it was his intention to control the institutions of government more thoroughly than they had ever been controlled before, so that all who could vote might be under no doubt of the road to reward. Although these aims were simple enough, their execution presented a problem of great complexity, involving intricate personal as well as public issues, but these were the years of Walpole's greatness.

Walpole had the ability to give his whole personality to the business in hand, so that his mastery of detail and his comprehension of contingencies were so much greater than anyone else's; in consequence, his policy usually prevailed. His capacity for work was abnormal; so was his energy, which never flagged. His appetite for power was as great as his industry, and his temperament and will, if anything, created the office of Prime Minister; the nation's business was sufficiently small for such an office to mean more than the chairmanship of a committee, or the vehicle of communication to the sovereign, or the figurehead of a party. Walpole was Prime Minister in the sense that his will dominated all aspects of the government's administration. He knew intimately all the government's servants, handled them personally, and was fully acquainted with the nature, extent, and detail of their business. If anyone threatened, as Carteret and Townshend threatened, his mastery, he worked with a steadfast purpose to eliminate them. To his subordinates he had a warm, human loyalty; to his rivals he was genial but implacable.

In 1721, Walpole had still far to go before he obtained absolute mastery of the government, nor did he know that chance would favour him. Within a year Sunderland was dead. Within the same twelve months, seven bishoprics fell vacant and they were filled with Townshend's and Walpole's nominees, all Whig, all loyal. France had a delicate boy-king, Louis XV, whose death might lead to a dynastic war, involving France with Spain, for Philip V was the nearest heir; although he had renounced his claim, renunciation meant little enough in the eighteenth century. England's friendship seemed urgently necessary to the French and, when they got hold of information of a Jacobite plot, they handed the evidence to Walpole. The leading Tory, the High Anglican Bishop of Rochester, Atterbury, was involved. He was exiled, and the stigma of Jacobitism firmly attached to the Tories, which for a time made them undesirable allies for any Whig group. The exposure of the plot, with the elaborate precautions which Walpole took to safeguard London, helped to restore a little the popularity of the government. The remains of the Sunderland group who were still in office grew perturbed at Walpole's increasing power and they searched for means to discredit him. This party was led by Carteret, a lazy, brilliant diplomatist who was Secretary of State. He had the support of the King's mistresses, both German, and his Hanoverian ministers, but he made the mistake of trying to please one mistress without considering whether the other, the Duchess of Kendal, the senior and more powerful, though the uglier, would be disobliged, a mistake in human understanding which Walpole quickly appreciated and exploited. Too late, Carteret

realized his folly and snatched at any opportunity to discredit Walpole.

Walpole had granted a patent to a Birmingham manufacturer, Wood, to mint copper coinage for Ireland. One of
the beneficiaries of Wood's patent was the Duchess of
Kendal. Seeing in this an opportunity for revenge, Carteret
intrigued with Irish Tories and discontented Whigs to in-
flame the resentment which the Irish had begun to feel,
stimulated by the biting sarcasm of Dean Swift's *Drapier's
Letters*. It was the end of Carteret as a political force. Walpole manoeuvred him into the position where he had either
to go to Ireland as Lord Lieutenant and settle the disturbance himself or resign and admit his responsibility. He went
to Ireland.

This, of course, finally destroyed the Sunderland group.
Everyone expected that Walpole would appoint William
Pulteney to the vacant Secretaryship of State. Pulteney was
a man of great verbal brilliance, but lazy, vain, and ambitious. He had few relations, and fewer clients, in politics.
Walpole passed him over and appointed the Duke of Newcastle – fussy, scatterbrained, but fabulously industrious, yet
so riddled with anxiety that decisions were painful to him.
Walpole had no intention that he should make any, for his
appointment was made partly so that Townshend could control foreign affairs. In the field of electoral patronage and
influence, Newcastle's wealth, industry, and astonishing
memory had created an unrivalled empire, and this was
the field which Walpole encouraged him to cultivate, and
through Newcastle the appointment to every office in
Church and State, no matter how small, was made con-
ditional on loyalty to Walpole. Of course, this bred resentment and grumbling amongst the unsuccessful seekers for
office, who found ready enough leaders in Pulteney and the
remnants of the Sunderland group, but Walpole was indifferent to the puny efforts of the ill-organized Parlia-

mentary opposition, for, with prosperity at home and peace abroad, the world was going his way.

The prosperity at home was aided by Walpole's financial and economic policy. At the Treasury he had a number of advisers of real ability with a flair for administration. With their help, Walpole reorganized the customs system; duties were removed from most exports and from the import of those raw materials needed by England's manufacturers, whose interests were preserved by careful protective legislation. The customs rates were simplified and reduced. In order to check smuggling and to encourage the development of London as a free port, excise and a system of bonded warehouses were introduced in 1723 for tea, coffee, and chocolate. This enabled them to be re-exported with little fuss and no expense to the merchant. With regard to the revenue he made a number of small administrative changes of great value. In none of these things was Walpole an innovator; but he had a greater mastery of the details of finance than any Prime Minister until Gladstone. It was in questions of administrative detail that he was most successful.

His long-term financial policy gave rise to bitter controversy, which lasted throughout the eighteenth century. The point of dispute was the attitude which Walpole took to the Sinking Fund. This had been instituted to make the public confident that the National Debt would be paid. It had this effect but, contingent on this, it had further effects which were not unforeseen. Confident that their money was safe, the investing public began to regard the National Debt as a gilt-edged security, a fact which Walpole quickly appreciated. With the growth of trade and the more efficient handling of finance, the taxes appropriated to the Sinking Fund produced far more than was anticipated and there was a possibility that the debt might be paid off more rapidly than was expected. At the same time, as we shall see, Walpole was faced by a number of demands for increased expenditure

which could be met only by increased taxation. Walpole
hated increased taxation. The most efficient tax was the
tax on land, for its yield was always predictable and it
was the easiest to gather (and so it was customary for extraordinary expenditure to be met by increasing it). On the
other hand, the Commons consisted of landowners and so
did the Court, and they, and Walpole with them, felt that
the land had borne the burden too long. The Sinking Fund
offered one alternative. Walpole raided it in 1727 for the
first time and then again in 1733. It is probable that he
never meant to use the Sinking Fund regularly in order to
meet current expenditure, but he was determined to relieve
the land of its burden of tax and, with the failure of his
Excise Scheme in 1733, he had no alternative. He had been
condemned both by contemporaries and posterity for it,
but the condemnation was short-sighted; the few millions
which Walpole might have paid off was insignificant compared to the burden of debt which the century's wars were
bound to bring.

However, there was an enforced break of six years in the
development of Walpole's economic policy which was
caused by a prolonged diplomatic crisis with Spain and by
the ministerial crisis to which this gave rise at home. In
1722 it had seemed that the differences between Austria
and Spain would be settled by a general European conference at Cambrai, in which England and France hoped to
act as mediators. By 1724 nothing had been achieved, and
Austria and Spain secretly discussed their mutual differences, which were resolved by the First Treaty of Vienna in
1725. The combination of Spain and Austria alarmed
France and England, and in England alarmed particularly
those merchants who feared that the Austrian Ostend Company might gain privileges in Spanish trade better than their
own. Townshend, reckless by temperament, was encouraged
by bellicose public opinion in London. By September the

Treaty of Hanover was signed with France and Prussia. This became the foundation upon which Townshend built an expensive system of alliances. By 1726 England was more or less at war with Spain.

Then Walpole began to exert himself. He disliked intensely the increased land tax which the foreign situation had made necessary, and he distrusted Townshend's attitude to foreign affairs, a distrust which is easy enough to understand, for Townshend was planning to divide the Austrian Netherlands with Holland and France and give England European territory once more. Walpole believed that, with France's help, Spain could be separated from Austria. It was not a popular policy, and commercial interests began to ally themselves with the opposition to Walpole. Indifferent to public opinion, Walpole went ahead. In 1729 he made the Treaty of Seville with Spain. Townshend lingered on in the ministry for another twelve months after the defeat of his policy. Finally, in 1730, he was replaced by Harrington, a client of Newcastle's, who for the time allowed the direction of foreign affairs to be Walpole's. In 1731 outstanding differences were settled with Austria in the Second Treaty of Vienna, and Walpole, having avoided war, was free again to pursue his long-deferred policy of financial reform to reduce taxation.

The years had proved that his most successful reform had been the introduction of excise for tea, coffee, and chocolate. It was true that they were still smuggled in enormous quantities, but the volume of legitimate trade had greatly increased and with it the revenue. In 1732 Walpole made it clear that he intended to extend this system of taxation. The public received the news with fury. Indifferent to clamour, Walpole went ahead and in 1733 introduced his scheme for excising tobacco; wine was to follow. For twelve months the opposition, under the skilled leadership of Pulteney and Bolingbroke, had carried on an intense publicity campaign against excise, which was universally detested. When the bill was before Parliament the Lord Mayor and Corporation created a formidable and well-organized opposition to it and threatened unconstitutional action if it were passed. Most historians have condemned this opposition as wilfully and deliberately factious, as un-principled exploitation of mass hysteria, by which a sound measure was destroyed to the country's loss. There is no doubt that the opposition exploited the situation to the utmost for its own political ends. There is no doubt that had the Bill been passed the revenue from the duty on wine and tobacco would have increased. There is also no doubt that had the Bill become law the liberties of the subject might easily have been endangered. Even with the modifications which violent opposition forced on Walpole, the Excise Bill would have created increased opportunities for patronage and increased administrative justice. This last to the public mind was the most sinister. In the eighteenth century there was little redress possible against officials of the Crown, and many of its minor officials were thugs and brutes who beat up their victims without compunction or stole or wrecked their property. The common man was at the mercy of the royal official and any increase in the power and authority of the State. When Excise was depicted as a monster swallowing and devouring ordinary men and women, it expressed a truth which seemed universal and self-evident. However, neither the apprehension of the public nor the violent demonstration of its dislike would have deterred Walpole. The implacable hostility of the Corporation of London, and its avowed intention to embark on unconstitutional action if the Bill were passed, weighed more heavily with him, though not so heavily as it did on those members of the ministry who had never been his friends – those Leicester House Whigs who had come into office in 1727, friends of the King when he had been Prince of Wales, who disliked intensely Walpole's supremacy at Court. They thought that they could use this crisis to get rid of Walpole, so they expressed hostility to the scheme at Court and in Parliament. Then, Walpole knew the game was up. He withdrew his Excise Bill, flattered the more powerful of his opponents and dismissed the rest. The Commons, realizing that he was master still, came to heel and switched their resentment to the City Corporation. Only the public rejoiced with wholehearted abandon.

CHAPTER NINE

SIR ROBERT WALPOLE AND THE PATRIOTS

1733-42

THE tide had turned. For over ten years Walpole had dominated the world of English politics. George II, and more
particularly his Queen, Caroline, had made his friends their
friends and allowed all the resources of the Household to be
used unsparingly in keeping his party loyal. From every crisis,
domestic or foreign, Walpole had emerged the victor, and
the full measure of his power at Court can be judged from the
fact that George II voluntarily laid aside all the outstanding
difficulties between his Hanoverian dominions and Austria
so that the Second Treaty of Vienna could be completed in
1731, for the failure of this Treaty would have marked the
failure of Walpole's own incursion into foreign affairs.

But Walpole's policy had bred distrust, his methods
hatred. Time and time again his policy was successful in
Parliament only because of the government's absolute control of the Scottish members in the Commons and the
Bishops in the Lords. It gave point to the opposition's cry
that Walpole's policy was against the wishes of the nation,
a policy imposed by a corrupt use of pension and place.
From 1726, under the inspiration of Bolingbroke, a brilliant
group of journalists had attacked Walpole in their paper,
The Craftsman, on these lines. In Parliament a strange alliance of Jacobites, Hanoverian Tories, and discontented
Whigs under Pulteney, hammering at the same theme, had
dangerously reduced Walpole's majority. Hated and opposed, Walpole was secure until 1733. Before then the

opposition was only a brilliant *tour de force*, infinitely adroit in its exploitation of discontent but never once a serious rival for political power. Its heterogeneous nature prevented that. A government containing Tories was impossible and there were not enough Whigs of sufficient electoral influence or ability to form a government. After 1733 this was no longer true. Chesterfield, Bolton, Cobham, and many another Whig peer had been cast out of office for opposing the Excise Scheme. A solid phalanx of Whig peers was ready to seize power if Walpole faltered or lost the confidence of the King. So large, so numerous, so brilliant a body of influential men naturally won the adherence of young, aspiring politicians, for both Walpole and the King were ageing. Not only were young politicians and the opposition well aware of Walpole's age, but so were his friends – Newcastle, Harrington, and Hardwicke. They were much younger than Walpole and they were concerned, of course, with their own futures and not with his.

Nor were the times propitious to Walpole. The question of the Polish Succession had brought war to Europe: George II, Caroline, and their Hanoverian advisers pressed for a war which Walpole knew would be far too unpopular to risk on the eve of a general election. As it was, he managed to keep out, but at a price. Newcastle, Harrington, and Hardwicke began to have their first doubts as to the wisdom of Walpole's policy, and without their continued allegiance Walpole's fall was certain. Then he was outwitted by the French, who concluded the Third Treaty of Vienna (1738) without England's knowledge. France's power and prestige were greatly increased by England's diplomatic isolation. The opposition prided itself on its patriotism. It desired glory and splendour for Britain, and the pacific policy of Walpole was regarded by them as a national humiliation.

At home, affairs went little better. Immediately after the Excise crisis Walpole had to prepare for a general election in 1734. With many influential peers in opposition, and with the memory of Excise still acute, Walpole and Newcastle had a desperate and costly battle, which they won only by their control of the smaller boroughs. In the counties and the big towns, anywhere where public opinion still counted for something in elections, they failed. As it was their majority was only fifty, a slender enough margin, which might disappear overnight at the first threat of a ministerial crisis.

The change in Walpole was marked. Instead of dominating men and circumstance, he was willing to temporize with both to preserve his hold on power. Previously he had been indifferent to public clamour or private animosity, but, after 1735, his first principle was caution and discretion. Economic and fiscal reform was over. A suggestion that the interest on the National Debt should be reduced from 4 per cent to 3 per cent was rejected. Rather than raise taxation, the Sinking Fund was raided year after year for ever increasing amounts. But life was turning against him. In 1736 Frederick, Prince of Wales, quarrelled violently with his parents, a quarrel which Walpole mishandled. The upshot was a rival court at Leicester House and a social centre for the opposition. The next year the Porteous Riots in Scotland, in which he deferred to public opinion, further lowered the prestige of the government at home. Then, in 1737, Caroline died. For ten years she had been Walpole's most loyal ally. In return for a little clerical patronage and the illusion of power she had worked with unmatched patience to get his policies accepted by the King. Frederick with a rival court and a rival government ready to take power, the Queen dead, Walpole hesitated to thwart the whims of the King, for in George's support lay his main, almost his only strength; without it, he knew that his friends of a lifetime would desert him without compunction; only so long as his capacity for handling the King made him valuable as an ally was it in their interest to support him.

Although the Third Treaty of Vienna settled the Polish question and gave France Lorraine, it did not bring lasting quiet to Europe. The new alliance between France and Spain – the Family Compact of 1733 – was viewed with great suspicion by many Englishmen, who felt that the French might usurp their commercial advantages which the Spanish Empire offered. For years past there had been a steady campaign of hatred towards Spain in which Spanish atrocities on English seamen played a prominent part. The Spaniards also resented the privileges conferred on the British by the Treaty of Utrecht – the monopoly of the Slave Trade to the Spanish West Indies and the right to send one trading ship each year to Vera Cruz. There were admitted rights and wrongs on both sides, which Walpole hoped to adjust by negotiation, and at first the Spaniards did not show themselves unwilling to compromise. In the eighteenth century negotiations with Spain were always long, laborious, and inconclusive. When at last the Convention of Prado was drawn up, it was denounced as a national humiliation by the 'patriots' both in Parliament and in the Press.

When Trade is at stake it is your last Retrenchment; you must defend it, or perish.

These words of Pitt's thrilled the nation, especially London; men felt that here was the authentic voice. Pitt did not flinch from the contemplation of the violent aggression required by an active and expanding commercial imperialism, and such an open avowal of England's aspirations bred its own elation. But equally important with this was Pitt's very genuine moral fervour. England's grandeur was the will of God. War was virtuous as well as necessary, and virtue would be rewarded with victories attended with something more solid than glory.

Sir, Spain knows the consequences of a war in America. Whoever gains, it must prove fatal to her.

As Burke said many years later, a war with Spain was a war of plunder – but it was also felt to be both necessary and righteous. Except by Walpole. He would never have given way to the clamour of the opposition and of the public, but he was once more faced with a ministerial crisis – and one much more serious than he had faced before. Newcastle was convinced of the necessity for war, and he was supported by Hardwicke, the Lord Chancellor, and by Harrington, the other Secretary of State. For years Walpole had dominated Newcastle and Hardwicke, and even when they had disliked his policy he had forced them to comply. This time, he failed. England went to war. 'It is your war,' Walpole said to Newcastle, 'and I wish you joy of it.'

There was little joy to be had of it. After years of peace the army and navy were badly equipped and incompetently manned. There were not enough ships to meet the demands of a naval war which covered the seas of the world. The little success achieved was due to individual brilliance and daring – the burning of Porto Bello by Vernon and the magnificent and adventurous voyage by Anson round the world. In general the war drifted on incompetently and expensively. After Frederick the Great's attack on Silesia, it was certain that sooner or later the war must involve all Europe. Yet Walpole was unable, and probably unwilling too, to take serious charge of affairs. His end was only a matter of time. The general election of 1741 reinforced those who clamoured for an active and vigorous imperialistic policy. Newcastle and Hardwicke hesitated no longer. They let it be known that they were prepared to countenance a coalition government which would prosecute the war vigorously. Walpole's day was done. He knew it and resigned in 1742; three years later, he was dead. The defeat of Walpole was more than the defeat of a man; it marked the passing of an age.

For twenty years Walpole had just held in check those

aspirations natural to a society which was faced with enormous possibilities of commercial expansion, a society which had, too, the capacity to seize its chances and the wealth and men needed to exploit them. Walpole had avoided war and kept the peace because he believed England existed for the sake of men of substance, who gained from security and low taxation, and not for the sake of rash commercial adventurers. Walpole's success was achieved with great difficulty. He survived one ministerial crisis after another only because he enjoyed the full confidence of the King and had the control of the Crown's extensive patronage. But in a sense he made too clear the sinews of government. He displayed how the Commons could be controlled by the Court, a lesson which was never forgotten. He dominated the political life of his time because, realizing the smallness and intimacy of political society, he was able to catch its members in a network of patronage and influence. By doing so he had brought the institutions of government into grave disrepute and so paved the way for the radical attack of the sixties and seventies; but, for the time being, having forced the government to accept their policy of aggressive war, Pitt and his associates were prepared to suspend their campaign against corruption and use the methods of Walpole and of Newcastle for their own ends.

England has never known a prime minister more adroit in handling men than Walpole, but he was too rooted in reality, too sensitive to the everyday world to be a great statesman. It was Chatham, ignorant of men, ignorant of politics, who knew with utter certainty England's destiny and showed her the way to it.

PART II

THE AGE OF CHATHAM

*

'In England it was an age of aristocracy and liberty; of the rule of law
and the absence of reform; of Lati-
tudinarianism above and Wesleyanism
below; of the growth of humanitarian
and philanthropic feeling and endeavour; of creative vigour in all the
trades and arts that serve and adorn
the life of man.'

G. M. TREVELYAN

CHAPTER ONE

THE AGRARIAN AND INDUSTRIAL REVOLUTIONS

1742–84

RECENTLY the words Industrial Revolution have come in for a great deal of abuse. It is true that the tempo of industrial life was already changing long before 1760, which is conventionally regarded as the beginning of this revolution, but to no discerning man of the time did it seem that this change in tempo would affect fundamentally the whole nature and structure of English society. Between 1760 and 1790 it was crystal clear that there were two worlds, the old and the new; the new was the product of technological change and certain of success, certain to bring into being a new and strange Britain. Nor could the process be gradual. To us who are used to violent and rapid changes, the rate of change may seem slow and, of course, it is possible in 1800, or even in 1850, to point to enclaves of old England whose ways of life would have been familiar to men of the sixteenth and seventeenth centuries. But, compared with the centuries which had gone before, the changes in industry, agriculture, and social life of the second half of the eighteenth century were both violent and revolutionary.

That this was so was neither fortuitous nor accidental. The age of Walpole had witnessed a very rapid expansion of British trade and the opening of new markets both at home and abroad. There was a demand for increased productivity and merchants had sufficient capital to spare to invest in industrial enterprise. But there was a shortage of labour and, although invention and better organization did something to overcome it, it remained a fundamental check on rapid expansion.

After 1740, however, there was a steady growth of population due to a marked, if small, decline in the death rate. Almost certainly this was due to improved midwifery – the product of the great Edinburgh school of medicine – the Hunters, Pringle, and Smellie, and to the foundation of lying-in hospitals and orphanages; the first kept the children alive, the second prevented them being exposed. This growth of population had a tonic effect on the British economy. It increased the home market, provided more labour, and swelled the growing, man-eating towns. Yet perhaps the most important effect was the survival of more children of the middle and lower middle class parents than ever before. This was the greatest stimulant of all. With some education, a little capital, occasionally an influential relative, the expanding world offered them endless opportunities of advancement. The early industrial capitalists – Watt, Wedgwood, Arkwright, Fielden, Peel, Wilkinson, and a score of others – all emerged from the lower middle classes. And, of course, there were hundreds who failed. But without a rapidly expanding lower middle class with sufficient education and technical background the Industrial Revolution would have been impossible. This and a growing labour force, adequate capital, and expanding markets were the prerequisites; they provided the opportunities to which human ingenuity and skill readily responded.

The most revolutionary developments were in technology, in transport, and in methods of industrial organization. Where in the early part of the century there had been one profoundly important invention which only gradually affected industry, now there were a dozen, and their diffusion, although slow by modern standards, was rapid by comparison with what had gone before. In textiles, Arkwright's water frame (1769), Hargreaves' jenny (1770), and

Crompton's mule (1779) revolutionized the production of yarn and brought to the weaver an age of golden prosperity which was to last for a quarter of a century. These improvements spread rapidly in the relatively young cotton industry, but in the woollen, where there were old-established vested interests, their adoption was delayed. In mining, metallurgy, and engineering the technical advances were greater and they affected the development of English industry more profoundly.

The problem of smelting iron with coal, successfully tackled by the Darbys of Coalbrookdale, was perfected by the Cranages, Smeaton, and Cort with their inventions in the reverberating, puddling, and rolling processes, inventions which made the productions of cast iron rapid and cheap. The great works of Carron in Scotland and Dowlais in Wales were started; and England regained her position as the foremost iron-producing country in Europe. Just in time, for England was to be at war for most of the century. Not only was iron produced in greater quantities, but new iron machinery brought greater control over material, which led to finer and more accurate work, so that the greatest of all ironmasters, John Wilkinson, believed that iron should replace wood and stone in every way. His faith in the possibilities of iron were boundless and, as he controlled the greatest ironworks in the country, he could test his faith. He produced railroads for mines (1767), built the first iron bridge in the world over the Severn (1779), built an iron chapel for Wesleyans, saw the first iron boat afloat (1787), and finally he was buried suitably in an iron coffin (1805). But Wilkinson was more than a man with iron fever; he had real genius for organization and a restless adventurous spirit – he had iron interests at Nantes and Creusot, wharves at Rotherhithe, tin mines in Cornwall, coal mines in the Midlands and his own canal, and iron lighters to shift the coal to his furnaces. No one had a quicker grasp of the industrial possibilities of an invention, and he was one of the first to realize the industrial possibilities of Watt's steam engine invented in 1769. He ordered one for power purposes other than pumping (1775), and, by using the very accurate methods he had developed for boring cannon, he provided Watt with cylinders which made the engine far more efficient. At first, of course, the use of Watt's engine was limited almost entirely to mining, as Newcomen's engine had been in the past. But in 1781 Boulton and Watt produced the improved engine with a rotary motion, and its use became more widespread both in England and abroad. With the perfection and adoption of a power engine, made of iron and steel and using coal, England had completed the first stage of a profound revolutionary process. Man was no longer dependent on the natural sources of power.

Adequate transport and efficient financial arrangements and a proper control of labour preoccupied the new industrialists as much, or almost as much, as inventions. By 1760 the improvement of river navigation had reached its limit, and Brindley and the Duke of Bridgewater showed the way round the impasse by cutting the Worsley canal (1761), and so halved the price of coal in Manchester. The lesson was quickly learned. In 1767 Manchester and Liverpool were joined; ten years later the Grand Trunk linked the Mersey with the Trent and brought a world market to Josiah Wedgwood at Etruria. Every canal cut cheapened goods, brought them within the reach of humbler classes, and raised their standard of life. Nor could men such as Wilkinson, Boulton, or Wedgwood tolerate the foul slow roads, for their widespread interests demanded speedy travel. They brought all their influence to bear on the Turnpike Trusts for a radical improvement of road engineering. In the sixties Trusts multiplied and, at last, a real attempt was made to grapple with the problem, but progress, although definite, was slow.

Nevertheless, the isolation in which most Englishmen lived was gradually broken down, and a network of stage coaches helped to bind the economic and commercial interests in a closer unity.

Inadequate financial methods and arrangements were as much an impediment to the early industrialists as bad transport. In the early years of the century there were no country banks, and large-scale financial transactions could take place only through London. London still, of course, maintained this supremacy, but the widespread development of country banks after the fifties made the development of industrial enterprise easier. Even so, there was never enough coin to meet the weekly wagebills of the great enterprises, and Wilkinson and others produced their own silver and copper coinage and guinea notes. They overrode difficulties with that simple confidence born of certain and continued success; they allowed nothing to stand in their way.

Above all, they kept a steady eye on their common interests and were willing enough to enter into combination with fellow capitalists to secure them. By 1777 the Midland iron-masters, led by Wilkinson, were holding quarterly meetings to fix prices and conditions of sale. Earlier still, in 1774, Manchester had what was in effect a Chamber of Commerce. But in 1785, Josiah Wedgwood achieved a long-cherished ambition when he formed the General Chamber of Manufacturers of Great Britain, which drew the scattered associations into one national body, through which Wedgwood hoped to influence government policy. Although not as successful as he hoped, it is true to say that this body, as well as the smaller associations, were powers in the land. Industry was no longer the handmaid of commerce but its mistress.

*

In agriculture the changes taking place in the age of Chatham can best be expressed in figures.

No. of Enclosure Acts per decade

1700–10	.	. 1	1750–60 .	. 156
1710–20	.	. 8	1760–70 .	. 424
1720–30	.	. 33	1770–80 .	. 642
1730–40	.	. 35	1780–90 .	. 287
1740–50	.	. 38	1790–1800	. 506
			1800–10 .	. 906

Average Weight of Cattle sold at Smithfield

				1710	1795
Oxen	.	.	.	. 370 lb	800 lb
Calves	.	.	.	. 50 lb	150 lb
Sheep	.	.	.	. 38 lb	80 lb

These figures express a profound revolution, both social and technical. The most fundamental change was the supersession of open by enclosed fields. The enclosure of fields and of common land had been going on steadily from the fifteenth century, but the face of England had hardly been changed. Between 1750 and 1780 the English countryside became the countryside we know, a countryside of hedges, fields, and scattered farms. The technical case for enclosure was exceptionally strong. It made each farmer independent of his neighbour, free to introduce improvements in crops and breeding without fear that his efforts would be wasted. Before, with land held in common and with herds mixing on the common pastures, improvement had been wellnigh impossible. Now the pendulum swung the other way and owners of rich, large estates were willing to try any experiment in what had become a fashionable cause. Many had a startling success. Coke of Holkham, on soil which had been regarded as too light for profitable farming, raised his rental from £2,200 to £20,000 a year in forty years. He did this by marling the soil and giving his tenants long leases but on very strict conditions which insisted on the most up-to-date methods of cultivation. He achieved European fame and became a model for gentleman farmers.

So did Robert Bakewell of Leicestershire, who pioneered the way in improved breeding of sheep and cattle. He changed English sheep, from the resemblance of a cross between a dog and a goat, to the plump, fleece-covered animal we know today. His success was due to intense in-breeding of animals having the points which he wanted. He used the same methods with equal success with cattle. New grass and root crops kept these herds alive during the winter, England was freed from the dreariness of salted winter meat, and the roast beef of old England soon became a legend. The new farming made another fundamental change in the people's diet. With the new soil techniques it became possible to grow wheat almost anywhere in England and everyone, including the poor, ate white wheaten bread, which if bad for their health was good for morale, for, like the consumption of roast beef and beer, it was regarded as one of the founda-tions of an Englishman's superiority over the French.

Yet, when considering the agricultural and industrial revolutions, there must always be many reservations. Every-where the old traditions and old techniques lingered on. Obstinacy, stupidity, and ignorance are common human failings, and so is aversion to change. Only in regard to enclosure did the State take any measures which tended to coercion, and these were always particular and never general. But the hold of the past had been weakened. Technical change, instead of being a rare event, had become a constant factor in human life. Since the neolithic revolution, when men learned to domesticate animals and grow crops, there had been nothing of such consequence for the material destiny of man.

CHAPTER TWO

THE SOCIAL CONSEQUENCES OF THE INDUSTRIAL REVOLUTION

PROFOUND changes in the economic life of the country must necessarily disturb its whole social structure, and the Industrial Revolution was no exception. Naturally, too, it bred a new attitude of mind to the old problems of society – poverty, crime, debt, disorder, and waste, and, of course, a critical attitude to the ancient and inefficient constitutional machinery which bore so little relation to the needs of society. Satire or self-satisfaction, the common responses of the Augustan age, were replaced by analysis and constructive criticism. But the most dominant note is a growing moral imperative, an insistence that human virtue can be measured only by its immediate social value, an attitude of mind which could justify both reform and repression.

This new moral outlook as yet scarcely touched the aristocracy. For them it remained a golden age of power, privilege, and increasing wealth. And they became a little intoxicated with it all. About many of their lives there is a touch almost of fantasy. Many felt no necessity for restraint and allowed their personalities full indulgence. The more they indulged themselves, the more separated they became from the hardening, purposeful world beneath them. The great Whig families – the Cavendishes, Russells, Bentincks, Manners, and the rest – still had great political empires to rule which gave them a natural position of authority in government. This political responsibility helped to keep the world of society on an even keel and saved it from the utter futility of its French counterpart, which it resembled more closely than most English historians have been willing to admit. There is the same grotesque extravagance, the same heightened class consciousness, the same feckless attitude to the crises in politics or society. The years before the wars with revolutionary France were the years of England's *ancien régime*.

Their luxury and *ton* still provoked envy and a desire to emulate amongst the squirearchy; and whichever sentiment dominated still tended to divide Whig and Tory squires. But there is no doubt that there was a weakening in political animosity. At times, as in the great Oxfordshire election of 1754, when the Tories spent £40,000 in an attempt to oust the Whigs, the old rancours could be as bitter as ever. But by and large the times were drawing them together. The problems of rural poverty were problems which touched all landowners, big or small. It is noticeable that, after 1750, the county aristocracy begin to attend the more important Quarter Sessions in order to formulate a common policy with their neighbouring squires. In the West Midlands and in the North a further threat was gathering about the leaders of the county. The new industrialists were interested in law, order, and efficient administration. In Lancashire it was an avowed rule not to tolerate any manufacturer as a colleague on the Bench. The threat of the new world was weakening the antagonism between old Whig and old Tory. They remembered that in the first instance they were gentlemen.

For decades rural society was able to resist successfully any attempted invasion of industrial capitalists, and almost the only county bodies upon which they secured positions of some authority were the Turnpike Trusts. But the towns were a much easier citadel to storm, for there they were backed by the more energetic and vigorous citizens, with whom they had many identical interests. As soon as the industrial towns ceased to be large, overgrown villages and became towns in a modern sense, the complete lack of local government and local administration became unbearable even to a people who loathed the hint of any restraint on their liberty of action. The government had absolutely no intention of touching local privilege and, where ancient corporations existed, it was inconceivable that they should willingly divest themselves of the immense privileges and profits which they enjoyed at the expense of their fellow citizens. Westminster, which had been deliberately given by Burleigh a weak and divided government so that it would never develop into a strong and powerful corporation like London, pioneered the way. A body of enterprising citizens between 1761 and 1765 secured Private Acts of Parliament by which they were enabled to levy a house rate in return for providing paving and lighting. They had the right to sue for the rate if any local anarchist refused to pay. This was the end of a long local struggle, and the improvement in social amenities at Westminster was startling. The lesson was well and quickly learned. Birmingham followed in 1769 and then citizens of town after town secured rights and powers to run social services in their towns. They went by a variety of names, Paving Commissioners, Lighting Commissioners, Improvement Commissioners, even Police Commissioners, for law and order was as rare as lighting, paving, and sanitation. On these bodies there was no distinction of creed, Catholic and Dissenter and Jew sat with Anglican, and newcomers to the town were more numerous than the old-established families. Time and time again these commissioners enlarged their field of operation and early in the nineteenth century the Manchester Police Commissioners were running the gasworks. This growth of local authorities is the most important social development of the second half of the eighteenth century and one of the least known and least stressed. Without it, the great administrative revolution of 1820–40 would have been impossible to accomplish. For one thing, it created a unity of interest between the administrative class and the new industrial magnates, intensified their belief in order, efficiency, and social discipline. It gave them a satisfactory outlet for their energies which did something to alleviate their impatience with the constitution. They became addicts of administrative reform and an easy prey for Bentham, but at least they were saved from the revolutionary doctrines of France. Above all, they fostered both social conscience and civic pride, which in their children and children's children became a part of the massive grandeur of Victorian Liberalism. Their immediate effect on English social life was tremendous. Both London and provincial towns for cleanliness and orderly living became the wonders of Europe.

From this everyone gained, the town middle class and the poor as well as the rich. By the end of the century most of the diseases of filth had been checked and diminished, if not destroyed, and in the nineties for the first time the birth rate in London passed the death rate. This steadily declined until the wholesale introduction of the water closet forced it up. Instead of being carried away to the country, excrement was swept into the Thames which provided London's drinking water. Typhoid returned. But this was a minor check, for every new development seemed to aid life instead of death. The improved food, the use of pottery instead of pewter, the widespread use of cheap cotton clothes which could be washed, the provision of water, the removal of filth and dirt from the streets, the foundation of hospitals, the increased knowledge of medicine all contributed to create a rapidly expanding population.

But a rapidly expanding population means a world of children. The children of the poor had always worked as soon as they could walk, but now their work was exceptionally valuable to factory owners. Children are tractable and easy to discipline; for simple repetitive operations they were ideal, and they were cheap. Naturally they had none of the ingrained antipathy to factory work common among adult workers. So the factories and the mines absorbed them; and child labour was more deliberately exploited than ever before. And, of course, it became much more visible. Children coming home from the factory or the mine stab the conscience which is at rest so long as the drudge is in the home or workhouse.* Between the stirring conscience and effective action stretched many decades.

Certainly, it was a hard world for poor children, but for their parents it is less easy to generalize. Probably they were healthier and certainly their standard of living was higher – at least in the towns if not in rural England. Nor did invention and the factory system quickly obliterate craftsmanship or the domestic system. Some inventions, like Hargreaves' jenny, could be used in domestic industry and, of course, the factory system spread slowly even in those industries, such as cotton and iron, where it had a natural advantage. Putting out and subcontracting were widespread, creating a large class of semi-independent, small-scale capitalists, almost one might say minute capitalists, men employing one or two workmen in a backyard shed. Even in the factories themselves skilled workers sometimes employed their own unskilled labour. And in almost every industry and craft the old domestic system vigorously survived. The worst conditions, long hours, irregular payment of wages, truck, gross exploitation of female and child labour were to be found in small-scale and domestic industry, for the profit margins were smaller but more essential, if the master was to struggle up the ladder of success. These hard conditions were partly compensated by greater individual freedom. The personal relation with the master, scarcely separated by class, was

*Agitation against child labour was not confined to the nineteenth-century humanitarians. One of the most visible and appalling exploitations of child labour in the eighteenth century was the chimney sweep. From 1760 Hanway and Porter carried on a campaign on their behalf and a Regulating Act was secured in 1788.

often intimate and there was a lack of discipline which no factory system could tolerate. Mondays and Tuesdays were often given up to drink, cock fights, bear baiting, and the other tough and brutal amusements of the poor, and the week's work would be done in a blind rush, in four sixteen- or seventeen-hour days. These were the workmen who viewed with deep suspicion the barrack-like factories whose long and regular hours savoured to them of the prison. And no doubt among many of the working classes the ultimate degradation was to become a factory-worker. Early trade unionism found its most fertile ground in the skilled and semi-skilled trades which bred this attitude of mind. It began very largely as a movement to protect privileges and to maintain established conditions of work. It was only much later that even rudimentary political interests were developed. The diversity of conditions of employment also prevented the growth of class consciousness amongst the workers and fostered in them a multiplicity of aspirations more personal than political.

For the poor who worked in factories life was bitter and hard. They had less of life's uncertainties, perhaps, than the lone worker and weathered hard times better, but it was a bitter life they led. Discipline in factories – especially with children – was harsh, frequently cruel. Living conditions were desolate and drab. And for most there was nothing to hope for. They were faced with the wearisome and endless repetition of a simple process, haunted by the fear of un- employment and starvation. Disease, poverty, fear, mal- nutrition, this was the common lot of our ancestors, and all the restless energies of the 'improvers' could not save them from it.

But salvation of a kind they found. It was provided by religion, by John Wesley. The industrial revolution paid no attention to parish boundaries. The mine ignored the parson. So that, by the middle years of the century, there

were scores of industrial villages and suburbs that were
without any church or priest. Ignorance of the most ele-
mentary facts of the Christian religion was astonishingly
widespread. Only a fundamental constitutional reform of
the Established Church could have coped with this situation, but such reform was unthinkable. for it would have
disturbed the entire structure of government. Dissent, too,
failed to realize its opportunities and obligations; for complex, obscure, and largely internal reasons, the old non-
conformist churches were moribund. It was left to Wesley
and his disciples to reap the rich harvest of neglected souls.

Wesley himself was a great and complex character, one of
the greatest known to modern times, a man in some ways
comparable to Luther, Lenin, Gandhi, or even Napoleon.
Few men have had his transcendental capacity to stir the
heart; none has combined this with his genius for organization. His greatness demands a separate chapter.

CHAPTER THREE

JOHN WESLEY AND THE ROAD TO SALVATION

JOHN WESLEY* was born in 1703 at Epworth in Lincoln-
shire, a younger son of the Rev. Samuel Wesley and his wife
Susannah. His father was a strong Tory, something of a poet,
vivid, courageous, highly and openly emotional, feckless.
His mother was also a Tory with an intense and deeply
personal religion, about which she thought unrelentingly
until its theological implications were as clear to her as the
simple rules of number. With unflagging determination she
imposed the pattern of her belief upon her numerous children. Her avowed intention was to 'break the child's will', to
impart Christian habits, especially industry and prayer; for
this end, at least once each week and with her help, her
children were taught to examine rigorously the state of
their souls. Her will power never faltered; her energy was
never exhausted; her intelligence never at rest. But love was
alien to her heart. She was proud of her children, ambitious
for them, but unmoved by their personal tragedies.

It is almost possible to label the qualities which Wesley
derived from each parent, for they were as contradictory in
him as they had been in their separate lives. He had his
mother's imperious will and her energy undiminished, but
also his father's craving for love, his passion for life. He
knew sin as his mother had never known it, but triumphed
over it with her qualities. It was at Oxford that Wesley
began his search for salvation. There he formed a Holy
Club with his brother Charles and fourteen others, amongst

*The best life of John Wesley is *Son to Susanna*, by Elsie Harrison
(Penguin Books 462).

whom was George Whitfield, who, as a popular preacher, later attained a reputation almost as great as Wesley's. In this club they practised austerities of outrageous proportions, which resulted in one member's death. They denied themselves food and sleep, and at night they prostrated themselves for hours in the winter frost. They spent their days in prisons and pest houses. This way of life attracted great notoriety, but it brought Wesley no sense of salvation.

He broke with Oxford and became a missionary to Georgia. Neither he nor his brother who went with him was a success. He fell in love, which seemed to destroy in him all self-control, and all sense of proportion. He was hounded out of the country. But he was nearer to salvation. He had met with a sect of Moravians and had been deeply impressed by their intense, personal religion. On return to London he continued to attend their meetings. On 24 May 1738, at Aldersgate, Wesley went through the great mystical experience which he described in these words.

I felt my heart strangely warmed. I felt that I did trust in Christ, Christ alone for salvation; and an assurance was given me that he had taken *my* sins, even *mine*, and saved me from the law of sin and death.

It was followed by no dark night of the soul such as the great mystics have known, but by a burning determination to bring to others what he himself had felt.

He was thirty-five, and, for the next fifty-three years, he travelled two hundred and twenty-four thousand miles and preached over forty thousand sermons, an average of fifteen a week. At first Wesley, who was, and remained, an Anglican, tried to work through the Establishment and preach in church, but, within a year, the Church became hostile and began to close its doors. Wesley was forced to preach out of doors. This was a blessing, for it brought him vaster audiences and took him to those savage villages and towns which lacked religion. Several times he was nearly martyred. He was never daunted. By 1784, in a span of twenty-five years, three hundred and fifty-six Methodist chapels had been built in places where there were practically no churches. Throughout the length and breadth of the land there were ever-growing, highly-organized bands of Methodists. The basic unit was the class, a group of about a dozen members living in the same locality. This class was controlled by a leader, appointed and not elected, who reported on the behaviour of his flock, their backslidings, weaknesses, and strengths. Larger than this were the bands which were themselves formed out of the society – the largest local unit. The bands were carefully subdivided according to sex, and then both sexes were again subdivided into married and unmarried. These groups practised communal confession of sins, exhortation, and prayer, and hark back to the Holy Club and Susannah Wesley's weekly examination of the soul. Each society had a steward who was responsible for collecting the donations which every Methodist was expected to make, no matter how poor, although in times of hardship and destitution money could be borrowed from the society. Periodically the societies were visited by Wesley himself or his lay preachers, helpers appointed by, and directly responsible to, him. All surplus funds of the societies were made over to Wesley and all buildings or property which they owned were in his name. Once a year the societies would send a delegate to the Annual Conference. It was not a conference for discussion or debate, but was held so that Wesley might criticize, exhort his followers, and declare his policy to his flock. The whole movement was strictly autocratic and Wesley's will and word were final. His enemies called him Pope John. By 1760 Methodism was easily the most highly coordinated body of opinion in the country, the most fervent, the most dynamic. Had it been bent on revolution in Church or State nothing could have stopped it. But then Methodism was not a religion *of* the poor but *for* the poor.

Both Samuel and Susannah Wesley had been Tories, and John had a profound respect for all established institutions. Methodists were expected to be Anglicans; they were encouraged to attend all the services of the Church, their Methodist practices being only additional to this. With the slightest amount of goodwill Methodism would never have become a separatist movement, but the implacable hostility of the Anglican hierarchy drove Wesley to the final and irrevocable step which made a breach inevitable. The spread of Wesleyanism in American made the need of ordained priests imperative. No bishop would ordain for Wesley. Finally he ordained his own and broke with the Church. But this was not until 1784.

In politics he was absolutely and completely conservative. He wrote: 'The greater the share the people have in government, the less liberty, civil or religious, does a nation enjoy.' He welcomed Parliament's attitude to Wilkes and regarded the French Revolution as the direct work of Satan. Political philosophers or radical thinkers he abhorred. For him the proper way to reform the evils of society was to transform the will of the individual. This was his plain truth for plain people. Wesley believed profoundly in salvation and rebirth, for that was the deepest experience of his own life, but, unlike the Moravians, he did not regard this as the final consummation of a religious life. Unlike Calvinist Whitfield, he did not believe salvation to be pre-ordained. Susannah Wesley had regarded the theological position of both Moravians and Calvinists as deadly dangerous, and she had insisted on Wesley breaking with both even at cost of splitting his own young movement. She saved Methodism as a social force for good works: a relentless, active, selfless Christian life became the Methodist ideal. Thrift, abstinence, hard work, and concentration were the essential virtues of those seeking salvation and those saved. The puritan ideal was reborn shorn of its political radicalism.

As a way of life, there can be no doubt of Methodism's appeal; it contained so much that was capable of satisfying the deepest needs of human nature. In the exercise of religion there was no emotional restraint. Sobbing, weeping, laughter, hysteria were commonplaces of Methodist fervour – a lack of restraint which seems to us almost pathological. But there was an edge to life in the eighteenth century which is hard for us to recapture. In every class there is the same taut neurotic quality – the fantastic gambling and drinking, the riots, brutality and violence, and everywhere and always a constant sense of death.* At no point did the Anglican or Dissenting churches of the day touch this inner tragedy of man, which was the emotional core of Methodism. But Methodism gave far more than emotional release; it brought a sense of purpose and a field for the exercise of both will and power.

To men and women who were just climbing out of utter poverty by the dint of their own thrifty endeavour this concentration of will and purpose was particularly appealing. The oligarchical and rigid nature of local institutions meant that there was little scope for ambitious men and women with a social conscience. All doors were closed to them, including, of course, those of the established Church, but Wesley provided an organization in which they could fulfil their need for power and their sense of duty.

Unfortunately, Methodism appealed to other, less socially valuable, sides of human nature. There was nothing intellectual about Methodism; the rational attitude, the most fashionable intellectual attitude of the day, was absolutely absent. Wesley believed in witches, in the coporeal existence of the Devil, and in possession by devils. He made decisions

*It was when Wesley preached of death and hell that his roughest audiences were most prone to convulsions and hysteria.

by opening his Bible at random and obeying whatever command he might discover from the first words which met his
eye. Wesley's superstitions were those of his uneducated
audiences. He produced a little book on physic which was
on sale at all meeting-houses. It is an absurd, fantastic com-
pilation of uncritical folk-lore. The leaves of the celandine
are to be placed under the foot as a cure for jaundice and
three pounds of quicksilver swallowed ounce by ounce will
untwist a gut. Everywhere in early Methodism one meets
the prejudices of the uneducated, which always seem to be
hardened by success. There was an anti-intellectual, philis-
tine quality which attracted the dispossessed but was dangerous for society.

It was at its worst in its attitude to education. Wesley considered play unworthy of a Christian child and, except to
produce lay preachers to carry on the good work, he was
uninterested in teaching. He considered a knowledge of the
Bible and of the Catechism sufficient education for any child,
and idle minutes he regarded as of the greatest danger to
the child's soul. For the sake of its everlasting life it ought
to be at work. Wesley more often than not was preaching
in districts with an ever-growing demand for child labour.
At the beginning of the century there had been a vigorous
movement for primary education, which, if supported and
strengthened by Methodism, might have survived the increased pressure from industry. But it got no support at all,
and education and the children suffered. The successful
Methodist could regard his overworked children with a
complacent heart.

In any violent religious fervour, intense hate as well as
intense love seems a necessary concomitant; Methodism was
no exception. It encouraged a violent hatred of Papists and
did all it could to maintain the laws against them. Jews were
the murderers of Christ. Any criticism which tended to cast
doubt on the literal interpretation of the Bible was the work

of the Devil. There was a rabid envy of luxury and elegance, of the aristocratic and libertarian attitude of life.

'To speak the rough truth,' Wesley said, 'I do not desire any intercourse with any persons of quality in England.'

Nor did his flock; the spirit was best preserved amidst the ugliness of suburbs and industrial villages through discipline and toil.

It was a strange quixotic mixture, a reactionary core in the most socially radical class; it strengthened those moral virtues which were to transform English society because they were fitted to economic needs and economic opportunities, and impelled willy-nilly a society with implicit faith in *laissez faire* to a closer knit social organization than mankind had ever known before. As Methodism came to judge human virtue by its social value, it lost its own soul in the pure fervour, the flame-like quality it gave to personal salvation. At 84, Wesley wrote:

The Methodists in every place grow diligent and frugal; consequently they increase in goods. Hence they proportionably increase in pride, in anger, in the desire of the flesh, the desire of the eyes, and the pride of life. So, although the form of religion remains, the spirit is swiftly vanishing away.

Few men have written a more dispassionate, or truer, epitaph on their own life work. But for the next five years he went serenely on, preaching, praying, exhorting, and his last words were: 'I'll praise, I'll praise.'

CHAPTER FOUR

THE ARTS AND SCIENCES OF
DR JOHNSON'S WORLD

OWING to the incomparable genius of Boswell, the massive, brooding figure of Dr Johnson dominates the intellectual life and culture of the middle years of the eighteenth century. His muscular intelligence never spared his weakest opponents: he would batter and bludgeon them so savagely that at times it is almost painful to read his replies. Yet his own character and beliefs were fissured with superstitions, fears, absurdities which at times reached the borderline of insanity. But by the sheer force and strength of his will, he has secured himself a unique position in English literature; he has become the intellectual John Bull for generations of Englishmen. He was truculent to the living, but no man had a greater respect for tradition. This, and his arrogant insularity, endeared him to his countrymen, who were facing the world alone and certain of their triumph. Yet, strangely enough, the greater part of Johnson's work belongs to the past, to the Augustan age of Swift and Pope. Fundamentally he lacked creative imagination, and he was more at home with literary techniques which were dominated by a strict sense of form. He had little sympathy with new tendencies in poetry and prose which were to give rise to the astonishing literary achievements of the romantic revival.

As yet there was little overt rebellion against the form and manner of the Augustan age. Gray drew the blinds of his coach to avoid the horrifying sight of the Cumberland hills; Cowper followed the master's footsteps and translated Homer. The slick, heartless, elegant phrases of the past still bespatter the poetry and denature the prose. But fortunately the leading writers of the day were not malicious, and so they were ignorant of the deadly intoxication of well-expressed malice. They were men of feeling – and of feeling too strong to be denied.

> To me the waves that ceaseless broke
>   Upon the dangerous coast
> Hoarsely and ominously spoke
>   Of all my treasure lost.
>
> Your sea of troubles you have past
>   And found the peaceful shore,
> I tempest-tossed and wrecked at last
>   Come home to port no more.

These words of Cowper are the authentic language of the heart, simple, deeply felt. Gray's *Elegy* has the same quality, so have the early poems of Burns. Gray's *Elegy* had immediate and overwhelming success; Burns' poems were eagerly sought as they were handed about in manuscript. The public was hungry for feeling, and, with that fine lack of discrimination which has always characterized the reading public, devoured the bad with the good, the bogus with the authentic, so long as they contained a faint echoing response to the demands of the heart. The *Poems of Ossian*, Percy's *Reliques of English Poetry*, *The Castle of Otranto*, and *Vathek* – the instant success of these indicates how strong was the public's craving for mystery and awe, wonder and fear. There was a growing discontent with the intellectual approach to literature; but discontent was not revolt. The mannerisms remained and the artificial conventions of writing were still worshipped. Garrick hacked Shakespeare to suit what he considered the taste of his age and his results were immediately admired – except by Dr Johnson, who would have preferred the plays left alone, and left unacted.

Drama had suffered most from its immediate past. In the

age of Walpole a certain life was to be found in the theatre
because it was a battle-ground for politics. Gay's *Beggar's
Opera* and Fielding's *Tom Thumb* were vigorous and powerful attacks on a government which most of London hated.
But after Walpole's fall the temperature of politics dropped
rapidly and the drama reached a pitch of dreariness unparalleled since *Gorboduc*. Dramatists concentrated on high
moral tone, pure sentiments, elegant diction: whether or
not their characters resembled human beings interested
them not at all. Wit was dangerous and avoided, and uplift
was regarded as more important than entertainment.
Bowdlerized Shakespeare, acted with Garrick's magnificent
power and range, was a welcome relief to the conventional
theatre. Such a state of affairs could not continue to exist
long, and at first Goldsmith with *The Good Natured Man*
(1768) and *She Stoops to Conquer* (1773), and then Sheridan
with *The Rivals* (1775) brought new life to the theatre.
Sheridan followed up his success between 1777 and 1779
with *The Critics*, *The School for Scandal*, and *A Trip to Scar-
borough*. He brought life and wit back to the stage and his
plays have never ceased to entertain.

A society of great wealth and stability always gives an
opportunity for painting – particularly portrait painting –
to flourish, but there is not always a genius at hand to take
advantage of his time. Sir Joshua Reynolds (1723–92),
between 1750 and 1780, painted the wealth and beauty of
England. He has no equal, if many rivals. His colour, line,
and form are incomparable and about his portraits of girls
there is a strange, liquid loveliness. Nor did he ever turn
away from the character of a sitter. His manner dominated
his time and influenced Thomas Gainsborough (1727–88),
George Romney (1734–1802), and Allan Ramsay (1713–84)
– painters of great technical ability, perhaps, save for Gainsborough, just short of genius – and many others who helped
Reynolds found the Royal Academy in 1768. These were

all, of course, painters of the fashionable world, but vice, violence, and poverty had their own genius in Hogarth. Hogarth was an exceptionally great painter, a creative artist to whom the social world meant very little. He could, and did, paint some wonderful portraits, but the main force of his genius was spent in bitter satire of the gross, social evils of his day.

Earlier in the century the wealthy had plundered the Continent to fill their houses with Italian fireplaces, French furniture and tapestries. The cult of the exotic was still continued and in Horace Walpole and his friends took a disquieting turn towards the Gothic, but these things affected only a little the broad trend of English taste. Taste was dominated by an extremely refined sense of proportion which craftsman after craftsman, famous or unknown, struck like a note in music – clear, precise, concordant. The great masters were James Gibb, William Kent, and the brothers Adam in architecture; in furnishing, first Thomas Chippendale and then Sheraton. They immortalized themselves and their time.

Science has always been more international than art, and this is demonstrated again and again in the middle years of the eighteenth century, especially in the investigation of problems relating to the nature of oxygen and electricity, and it is difficult to disentangle the work of English from that of continental scholars. The greatest English scientist of the time was Henry Cavendish (1730–1800), the grandson of the second Duke of Devonshire, and he made contributions of the first magnitude to both the great problems of eighteenth-century science – the separation and identification of gases and the nature of electricity. Unfortunately Cavendish was extremely eccentric. He rarely spoke; sometimes he did, and sometimes he did not, communicate his discoveries to the Royal Society. Some of his best work remained unknown for a hundred years and Faraday had to discover independently much that he had done. Apart from Cavendish there is no one comparable to Joseph Priestley – a strange polymath. Priestley's scientific work was done largely as an amusement, for he considered his philosophic, theological, and historical speculations to be his life-work upon which his claims to fame would be founded. He was a radical. He supported Wilkes, the American colonists, and the French Revolutionaries. His religious views were equally advanced. His notoriety was enormous, and many people, like Dr Johnson, regarded him as a menace to society. The Birmingham mob tore down his house and wrecked his laboratory. It would seem that Priestley had ample justification for his belief that he would be remembered principally as a philosopher. But, even in his own time, his experimental genius was building up a solid scientific reputation.

The work of our two most distinguished scientists – Priestley and Cavendish – rested, of course, upon the discoveries and methods of earlier workers. The Rev. Stephen Hales had invented, in 1727 or before, a satisfactory method of collecting gases, a fundamental step which made the investigations of Cavendish and Priestley possible. But Hales never seems to have investigated systematically the gases which he collected. The first person to do this was Joseph Black, the Professor of Chemistry at Glasgow. Black, too, was a man of genius, and he introduced for the first time quantitative methods, and brought strict and accurate measurements to chemistry. His methods and Hales' apparatus led to the isolation and investigation of carbon dioxide, which he called 'fixed air'. The unique position which chemists had always given to atmospheric air was no longer tenable, and it was not long before the nature of air itself was being investigated. Progress was, however, very seriously retarded by the assumption that metals were compounds of metallic earth and a mysterious substance called phlogiston. Although this theory did not by any means meet all the known facts, its adherents clung to it with the tenacity of martyrs. When on 1 August 1774 Priestley isolated oxygen he shattered the phlogiston theory, but so great was his faith that he refused to believe his own experiments and elaborated the most extraordinary reasons to make his facts fit the phlogiston theory. But later in the year Priestley dined with Lavoisier, the great French chemist, who immediately realized the significance of Priestley's discoveries. He shut himself up and worked fantastically hard until the following Easter, when he destroyed the phlogiston theory once and for all and established oxygen. He made no acknowledgement whatsoever to Priestley, who continued to hold to his own theory in the face of all evidence until his death in 1804. Meanwhile, in monk-like seclusion, Cavendish absorbed these discoveries and carried them further. He broke down water into oxygen and hydrogen, and so destroyed another of the age-old 'elements'. For once, Cavendish conveyed his discovery to the Royal Society. He also isolated the rare gas – argon – from the atmosphere: but this he kept to himself.

In physics, as in chemistry, the most fundamental discovery of the century was made by Priestley, but, again, it was a Frenchman who gave the discovery its final precision. In 1766 Priestley discovered the Law of Inverse Squares, that the attraction or repulsion between two electric charges is inversely proportional to the square of the distance between them, which became the starting point for the more precise work of Coulomb. Cavendish, too, was interested in the properties of electricity, and his investigations were of outstanding brilliance and absolutely fundamental, but such vital conceptions as potential and specific inductive capacity he kept to himself. Faraday rediscovered them in the middle of the next century.

But electricity was also a fashionable game. Louis XV

witnessed the administration of an electric shock to a line of monks a mile long and was convulsed with laughter when they all leapt into the air. Public demonstrations of the powers of electricity became exceedingly popular and profitable. To see brandy ignited by a spark shooting from a man's finger became one of the wonders of the age. Wesley became a firm believer in electricity's curative powers because he regarded it as a kind of *élan vital*, and he warmly recommended intense and prolonged electric shocks for a wide range of diseases from malaria to hysteria. Other amateurs preferred to experiment on themselves first and a miscellaneous crop of discoveries followed – the Leyden jar, Galvani's frogs' legs, and the great Anglo-American contribution – Benjamin Franklin's lightning conductors which George III had installed in Buckingham Palace as soon as he bought it.

There was a deepening curiosity about nature, about mankind, about society, and its historic past. In all studies there was greater precision, and an increased reliance on observation, a growing detachment from the intellectual attitudes of the past. There had been great works of historical scholarship before Gibbon's *Decline and Fall of the Roman Empire* (1776–88), but few historians had dared to display Gibbon's confident, self-reliant judgement, so precisely detached from traditional beliefs. There is the same unwillingness to accept popular superstitions, and popular beliefs, in Adam Smith's *Enquiry into the Wealth of Nations* (1776), which established political economy as a social science, whereas before it had been little better than ill-substantiated special pleading. Apart from such outstanding men as Gibbon and Smith, there were scores of other men of great ability, exploring or indicating new worlds of knowledge and understanding. And yet this wealth of science and art and scholarship was produced by a population far less than that of present-day London.

CHAPTER FIVE

CHATHAM AND THE DRIVE
FOR EMPIRE

THE fall of Walpole did not lead to the collapse of the
political machine which he had controlled for twenty years.
And some of the venom with which he was attacked by the
Tories may be attributed to their frustrated rage. The re-
arrangements which followed Walpole's resignation were a
deal between political bosses in which the interests of the
nation and the clamours of the public were scarcely regarded. For years the opposition had raged against seven-
year Parliaments, the tied votes of place-holders, and gross
corruption at elections. This attack was the one idealistic
feature of early eighteenth-century politics, the only political programme which could appeal to men with a sense
of moral purpose. But the programme was betrayed. Bills
for the repeal of the Septennial Act and for the exclusion of
placemen were thrown out as readily by Walpole's succes-
sors as by Walpole himself. It brought the realization that
the great hopes raised by the Revolution of 1689 were un-
likely to be fulfilled, so long as England retained its constitution unreformed. From 1690 to 1742 men of good will had
supported an attempt to purify the institutions of government, even though their leaders had been either political
careerists or, like Bolingbroke, tainted with a Jacobite past.
This moral purpose had been the great strength of the Tory
party and of the combined opposition to Walpole. But only
the crassly stupid, or the crassly obstinate, could support
such a policy after the experience of the forties. There was a
steady growth of the feeling that Parliament was debased
and rotten, and did not represent the power of the nation.

This feeling was particularly acute in London, but it was held in check partly by war and partly by Pitt. So long as he was in office the City felt that their interests would not be betrayed, and they continued to accept an institution for which they had little but contempt. Also, of course, the City was exceptionally prosperous: cynicism and toleration of institutional absurdity come more naturally to a wealthy society.

In one thing, at least, the new government was willing to gratify public opinion, and that was in a more ardent prosecution of the war. It was by relinquishing foreign affairs, in fact if not in theory, and sticking sensibly enough to the disposal of patronage that Newcastle had secured a compromise government. This, at least, prevented the wholesale proscription of the Walpole-Pelham block. Much to the King's delight, Carteret took over the virtual control of foreign affairs. He returned at once to the policy which had ruined Stanhope and Townshend – the full participation by England in a continental war. Alliance followed alliance with bewildering rapidity, and money poured into the pockets of German princes with troops to hire. Taxes rose. To each new situation, and each more disastrous than the last, Carteret had an answer which involved manoeuvres of infinite complexity in half the courts of Europe, and courts in the 1740s were numbered by the score. Taxes rose higher; and there was no success. Walpole, in retirement at Houghton, bestirred himself and pressed the King to dismiss Carteret. George wept bitterly when, at last, they parted; Carteret settled down complacently, and at once, to books and drink, which seem always to have given him as much gratification as, if not more than, diplomacy.

George refused to have Pitt, who had denounced Carteret's policy as a wild waste of England's resources for the sake of the 'despicable Electorate'. But 1745 was even more disastrous than anything that Pitt had forecast. French armies, led by the Maréchal de Saxe, Europe's best general, soundly defeated the English army at Fontenoy. French support of the Pretender had raised Jacobite hopes to a fever of expectation and, without waiting for help, Charles Edward had landed in Scotland. The Highlands had rallied to him.

There was a great deal of discontent in Scotland. The Union had brought prosperity for prosperous landowners with good land to farm and for Glasgow merchants in the Plantations trade. But, for crofters in the Highlands and for the small craftsmen in the Lowlands, the Union had brought increasing poverty. Also, many of the minor Scottish aristocracy envied and distrusted the way of life of the English aristocracy who despised them, and never bothered to conceal it. To these old-fashioned Scots the worldliness of the Hanoverians had degraded the function of kingship, debauched it for guineas, and, whether successful or not, there was a deep satisfaction in the affirmation of monarchial belief by the devotion to the Stuart cause. Charles Edward was built on heroic lines and, for once, the Jacobites had a royal leader who approached their ideal of kingship. It gave a vigour and a spirit to the movement which carried it to successes out of all proportion to its real strength. Charles Edward captured Scotland; invaded England and reached Derby. But England did not want the Stuarts, for the Stuarts meant subservience to France, followed by a decline in trade, and the threat of an alien religion. No Englishman of importance joined Charles. And, although there was a run on the Bank of England, there was no sign of panic. The inevitable end followed – retreat, defeat, flight. The Highlands were remorselessly, and finally, conquered and, as the years passed, they became a barren waste. But Charles Edward had been their one moment of hope, and, as despair deepened, he became an heroic, almost legendary, character, comparable almost to King Arthur, for in myths defeated nations can find consolation.

One man gained from the '45 – Pitt. The obdurate King was forced to give way and, in 1746, Pitt entered the government. The background of Pitt's life is as important as the background of Walpole's in our understanding of his political success. Unlike Walpole, Pitt was not born into a solidly established, centuries old, landed family, exercising traditional authority and political power. The family's fortune had been made by Pitt's grandfather, 'Diamond' Pitt, – a typical, buccaneering, East Indian merchant who began life as an interloper in India and finished as the Governor of Fort St George, Madras. 'Diamond' Pitt was tough, brutal, choleric, capable of immense rage, but he had such weight, such energy and vigour, that his leadership and authority were universally accepted. 'Diamond' Pitt, also, had great faith in his own life and career. He believed that the wealth and greatness of England depended on men like himself, ready to fight for a fortune in alien lands. Pitt was his grandfather's favourite grandchild, in fact the only one, for 'Diamond' Pitt usually referred with contempt to his 'unfortunate and cursed family' or the 'cockatrice brood of Pitts'. As far as his lonely personality would allow, Pitt was at home with men like his grandfather, men who believed that England's greatness and prosperity depended on aggression, on seizing and holding on to the world's trade.

But Pitt, too, had great gifts. He had, except for his own family, little humanity, none of that warmth and subtlety in human relations which was the foundation of Walpole's power. He had a much rarer and more effective gift – he could create the sense in all who listened to him that he was the mouthpiece of destiny. The controlled wildness of his temperament gave a passion to his oratory which hypnotized criticism and stirred profoundly not only Parliament but the nation. He was the first politician England had known whose power rested on the magic symbolism of his own personality and beliefs. But, of course, the power was intermittently used – it needed disaster or victory to call it forth. Although Pitt had little capacity for consistent work,* he had considerable originality, and a freshness of approach to strategic problems which overrode convention to a remarkable degree. Yet, against these positive gifts, there were alarming weaknesses of temperament which worsened with the years. He was a manic depressive, at times, especially in later life, out of his mind. He was obsessed with delusions of grandeur which bred a cold *hauteur* and disdain, which infuriated his colleagues, and made him almost impossible to work with. With success, he posed and postured to such a degree that many doubted his sincerity. All these things were faults of his unstable temperament, and it should be realized that Pitt was ill, physically and mentally, every year of his life. Without his passionate egoism, 'I know that I can save the country and that I alone can', without his profound sense of mission, his life would have been unbearable. In the rage and storm of politics and war, he was fighting for his own life.

*

It is necessary to consider his achievements and the causes of his final failure, and to understand what he had to offer to the hard-headed practical men who supported him. Fundamentally, Pitt's policy is easy to grasp. In the late thirties and early forties Pitt had spent much time studying the statistics of French commerce and industry, which had bred the conviction that France was the greatest danger England had to face, and the only rival worth considering in the race for overseas trade, and especially so when associated with the moribund hulk of the Spanish Empire. Two aims, he thought, should dominate English

*Pitt was a surprisingly efficient and orderly administrator but, of course, his work suffered from the long absences caused by his madness and ill health.

policy – supremacy at sea and the capture of French trading posts. As early as 1746 he was in correspondence with William Vaughan, a buccaneering fish merchant of New Hampshire, whose imagination had been fired by the capture of Louisburg, which dominated the mouth of the St Lawrence. Vaughan quickly realized that Quebec was the key to Canada. Pitt agreed. The reasons why Pitt wanted an attack on Canada were set out in a memorandum, sent by the Duke of Bedford, with Pitt's approval, to Newcastle. It contained five points, and their order is interesting and significant. They were:

1. The conquest would secure the entire trade in fur and fish.
2. The French would be prevented from supplying their West Indian islands with lumber, which would drive up the price of French sugar, to the advantage of our sugar merchants.
3. France would lose a market for manufactures.
4. France would no longer be able to build ships in America or acquire masts and timber. Their naval armament would be limited.
5. The expulsion of the French would give security to British North American colonies.

The last point carried the most weight with Newcastle, but not enough. He was haunted by the increasing cost of the war, which had led to a sharp increase in taxation, with consequent grumbling from the landed interest in Parliament. To embark on a costly expedition which would gratify neither the King nor Parliament, but only a handful of merchants in America and London, seemed folly and waste to Newcastle. The project was dismissed, but carefully preserved by Pitt.

Pitt accepted Newcastle's decision calmly. The war in Europe was dragging on, but obviously dying. A continuing war had few attractions for the public at large, unnerved as they were by the Jacobite successes. And Pitt himself was displaying a rare caution in the handling of his career. As Paymaster of the Forces, he had ostentatiously refused the traditional perquisites of his office. This had given him immense popularity in the City. But that was his only gesture. He worked with efficiency to improve the conditions in the army and, by doing so, hoped that he would soften George II's hatred, for the King doted on his army. His efforts were in vain. Pelham, Newcastle's brother – the Lord of the Treasury and Leader of the Commons – died in 1754. In the consequent reshuffle, Pitt expected high office and the leadership of the Commons. He obtained neither. He retired and waited. War with France – the Seven Years War – broke out in earnest in 1756. After a year's manoeuvring Pitt at last succeeded in obtaining what was in effect the sole direction of the war with the leadership of the Commons.* Domestic policy, that is raising money and maintaining the government's majority, was left to Newcastle, who was happy, if distraught, bearing his old familiar burden – attempting to gratify ten people with two places.

Until 1761 Pitt dominated the cabinet as far as the prosecution of the war was concerned. He chose commanders and planned operations, exercising an authority over the armed forces far greater than any other politician had enjoyed. From disastrous defeat Pitt led the country to sublime success, or so it seemed to him and his ardent supporters in the City; others had their doubts.

Pitt used the methods in which he had always believed. The use of sea power was the key to his strategy. His aim was to blockade the French fleet in Brest and Toulon, while a series of carefully-planned combined operations

*The intrigues between factions are too tedious to be related in a book of this size. Those interested will find an admirable account in Basil Williams' *The Whig Supremacy*.

destroyed, *not* the French empire, but French trade. Pitt was not interested in empires, he was interested in trade and paying for the war by capturing its most lucrative branches. In this he had the complete support of the City, whose merchants supplied him with intelligence about the nature, value, and location of the French gum, fur, fish, and sugar trades. By this method both Pitt and the City believed they could afford to pay both the immense subsidies which our continental allies demanded and the cost of those diversionary attacks on the French coast which Pitt conceived as necessary to his strategy. But it was the capture of trade which haunted his imagination and which to him and his City supporters made the whole struggle a matter of life and death for England. Trade was wealth and power. The only rival was France.

There were four theatres of trade – North America, the West Indies, Africa, and India. North America meant the control of fur, fish, and naval supplies. The strategy of attack had been worked out many years previously in consultation with American merchants. The capture of Quebec and Montreal was sufficient to capture the trade of Canada. Louisburg was reduced by Wolfe in 1758. Canada was open to attack. James Cook was sent to make a detailed survey of the St Lawrence river – a survey carried out with superb efficiency and thoroughness. Nothing illustrates Pitt's grasp of the realities of naval war better than this survey of Cook's, for, without the knowledge which it brought, Wolfe's task would have been doubly difficult. Wolfe, chosen by Pitt himself, had the temperament which cared so little for life that immense risks were taken, almost carelessly. The results were heroic – the scaling of the Heights of Abraham, the capture of Quebec, death and immortality for Wolfe. In 1760 Montreal followed Quebec. The fish, the fur, the naval stores were all ours.

Elsewhere there was equal success but, except in Africa,

less unity of purpose. About the West Indies, the City was divided. Beckford, the city millionaire, who was one of Pitt's most ardent supporters, regarded the capture of French sugar islands as likely to produce a glut of sugar, and reduce the price. Pitt believed that America could easily absorb the surplus, once the trade between Guadeloupe and the American colonies had been freed. Pitt got his way, and he was right. Guadeloupe was captured, and within a year Guadeloupe's customs duties had risen by 50 per cent, and paid for the expedition sent against it. In these years everything Pitt touched seemed to bring victory and profit. Dakar, with the gum and slave trade of Africa, was captured in 1759. Eyre Coote and Clive were winning such massive victories in India that Pitt left them to their own devices and concentrated on capturing the channels of oriental trade. At Mauritius, Pitt had his one failure, but this was wiped out by the brilliant attack on Manila, perhaps the greatest naval and military achievement of the war, and one which brought the control of the China trade in tea.

France was forced to risk her fleet in an attempt to break the blockade. In 1759 both the Toulon and the Brest fleets put to sea. Boscawen caught the Toulon fleet at Lagos and smashed it. Hawke took tremendous risks on the gale-lashed Brittany coast to destroy the Brest fleet in Quiberon Bay. Not since Blenheim had England been so overwhelmingly victorious. The memory of it has intoxicated posterity, but contemporaries were sober. They rang their bells; swarmed to Westminster Abbey and St Paul's to honour their heroes and their dead. There was gratitude that the dark days of '56, when defeat seemed near, were past. But there was doubt. To defeat France utterly, to despoil her of her trade and empire, would these actions not lead inevitably to further war and to a grand alliance of European powers against our overbearing greatness? Many questioned themselves in this way: others were frightened by the cost, by the increasing load of debt, and by the mounting taxation. The City was enriched, trade and industry were flourishing, and, even though the landowners shared the general prosperity, the tax which they bore grew heavier.

Newcastle was never good at formulating a policy; he was a man of bits and pieces. He was always at his wits' end to find money for Pitt's campaigns or Pitt's subsidies. When he heard the opposition's arguments against his financial policy, he was half convinced. Nor would Pitt bring the war to an end. In 1761 he insisted on war with Spain. But the old King had died in 1760, and his grandson listened attentively to those who doubted the wisdom of following Pitt. Also, the new King hated his grandfather's servants and intended to get rid of them. In the question of war with Spain, it was easy to split the ministry and to drive Pitt out and close the war.

But the Peace, not signed until 1763, enraged Pitt and enraged his City friends. It destroyed their grand conception. The sugar islands – Guadeloupe and Martinique – were given back, so was Dakar and the gum trade. Worse still, the French were given their old fishing rights on the Grand Banks, off Newfoundland. Without the fish trade, Pitt considered it useless to hold Canada. Only in India was anything saved. Sick, exhausted, unable to walk without help, or speak without stimulants, Pitt denounced the wreckers of his work for three wearying, weakening hours in the Commons' debate on the Peace. The burden of his speech was that 'we retain nothing, although we have conquered everything', and, in words which afterwards seemed prophetic, he phrased the guiding principle of his policy.

France is chiefly, if not solely, to be dreaded by us in the light of a maritime and commercial power: and therefore by restoring to her all the valuable West India islands, and by our concessions in the Newfoundland fishery, we have given her the means of recovering her prodigious losses and of becoming once more formidable to us at sea.

The City (but not the Commons) was impressed. In the previous year, at the Lord Mayor's banquet, they had insulted the King by the warmth of their acclamation of Pitt. His world and their world were one; he voiced, as no one else could, their aspiration, and he had given a moral purpose to their appetite for wealth, power, and dominion. All seemed within their grasp, but they failed, because they lacked political power. In defeat, they directed their attention to the institutions and methods of government. The day of the bourgeois radical dawned.

CHAPTER SIX

GEORGE III AND JOHN WILKES

THE intentions of George III in 1760 have been the subject of controversy for nearly a hundred years. The Whig historians of the nineteenth century created the myth of the Patriot King, of a monarch bent on restoring what he considered the usurped powers of the Crown and ruling through his friends. Behind the King are featured the sinister figures of the King's mother and her lover, the Earl of Bute, preaching the doctrines of Bolingbroke and goading the King to action which was unconstitutional by convention if not by law. Inept, obstinate, rash, tainted with madness, the new monarch went from tyranny to tyranny and from disaster to disaster, until the loss of an empire, and overwhelming defeat in war, brought the nation to its senses. With prophetic insight, the public insisted on the twenty-three-year-old William Pitt governing, as Prime Minister, on constitutional principles, immortalized by Burke. The mediumistic powers of the national mind were justified by Pitt saving us from Revolution, and by the recovery of the Empire, won by his father, but lost in the years of betrayal. Distorted nonsense as it is, it contains a truism. George III rowed ineptly and unavailingly against the tide of life.

Throughout the eighteenth century the heir to the throne naturally attracted dispossessed politicians, groups, and factions, based largely on family connexions, and, as the monarch aged, professional careerists and younger men looked hopefully to the heir, who might put them in power when he inherited the Crown. It was the pattern of a political life which was narrow, confined, limited to a small class

of society, which knew nothing of disciplined political parties, pledged to a parliamentary programme. Office, and not
the power to rule according to stated political principles,
was the aim of most eighteenth-century politicians. But
George II had lived a very long time, and he was a man
obstinate in his attachments, even if they were devoid of affec-
tion. He had been content to use the great Whig families –
the Devonshires, the Pelhams, the Townshends, the Russells, and the rest. To them he had delegated the immense
patronage of the Crown to use in the way Walpole had
taught them to use it. Peace or war, with only minor adjust-
ments and occasional crises, the system had worked, and
lasted, and the same families had produced regiments of
placeholders and ministerial voters. But their good fortune
had bred envy; long starved, the appetite grew wolfish,
especially amongst those, such as Bubb Dodington, who
had, at one time or another, tasted the sweet delights of
office. When George III succeeded, it seemed perfectly
natural to everyone that Bute, his tutor and closest friend,
should become Groom of the Stole with a seat in the cabinet.
Nor was Bute's meteoric rise to the Treasury any less expected. It was the end of the Pelhams and the constellation
of oligarchs associated with them. Nothing could save Newcastle, although he abjectly clung to office. He had made, and
translated, Bishops for nearly forty years, but they left him
in a drove for their new masters. Friends of a lifetime deserted him without compunction; his electoral influence,
the greatest England had known, and one upon which he
had dissipated an enormous fortune, melted rapidly away.
The last lines which he wrote were these:

It was myself, and I may almost say, myself alone, who rescued
the county of Nottingham, and all the boroughs in it out of the
hands of the Tories ... What would all my old county friends say
if they were alive, to see me upon the point of being drove out of
the county by two such ungrateful young men?

The ungrateful young men were the Duke of Portland and Newcastle's own favourite nephew, the Earl of Lincoln. The recipient of the letter, his election agent for thirty years in Nottingham, had also deserted him. It was easy to wreck and loot the great Pelham empire, but it was harder to build another. For ten years George was forced to use one make-shift ministry after another, until at last effective cohesion was achieved under the leadership of Lord North.

A change so great could not be based on personal issues alone, although they were of far greater weight and import-ance than many historians have realized. George was com-pletely devoted to Bute, and he adopted Bute's traditional Tory attitude to foreign affairs. His attitude to Hanover was as harsh, and as bitter, as that adopted by Chatham at the outset of his career. He referred to Hanover as 'that horrid electorate which has always lived upon the very vitals of this poor country'. To break the treaty relations with Frederick the Great, our major continental ally, was an act of patriotism. At all costs the war had to be stopped. Nor in the country at large, if we remember that the country at large was still the country of country-gentlemen, was such a policy unpopular. It was only in London, and in the great trading towns, such as Bristol, Liverpool, and Hull, that the royal policy was viewed with bitter distrust.

It was over foreign policy that George III and John Wilkes first clashed, giving rise to a struggle during which some of the most fundamental liberties of the individual in relation to the State were established. But to understand the success of Wilkes, and his symbolic popularity, it is necessary to consider certain aspects of social history. Between 1750 and 1770 considerable acceleration took place in the rate of economic and social change. London became a metropolis in a modern sense and many provincial towns ceased to be overgrown villages; they became provincial capitals. With this growth of population went growth in wealth, and wealth brought education and culture. The growing complexity of trade and technology called for a high degree of literacy, both in clerks and artisans, which in turn created a large newspaper-reading public throughout the country.* Improved communications enabled London news to be printed in Liverpool within two days and Liverpool papers followed the struggle between the King and Wilkes with keen interest. By 1768 there was a well-established Conversation Club at Liverpool which met weekly and debated general, and specific, political questions. One week, they debated – under what conditions was a man most free? Another week, whether political liberty could possibly be achieved in England without the introduction of the ballot box. This argues a hitherto unsuspected political awareness in the provinces, which helps to explain the support given to Wilkes, to the cause of the American colonies, and to the radical movements of the seventies. It also meant that the sudden change in foreign policy was discussed by men not only accustomed to political debate, but already organized for political action. It was a natural step for Conversation Clubs, and the like, to pass resolutions, to communicate letters to the Press, and to subscribe to Wilkes' campaigns.

John Wilkes belonged to the *nouveaux riches*. His father was a wealthy Clerkenwell distiller who had married him to an aged heiress. His youth was narrow, dismal, confined, but Wilkes had a naturally ebullient temperament, and, as soon as he had money enough, he slid easily into a gay and dissolute world where his superb verbal wit and amiable effrontery were appreciated. But the change from virtuous middle-class domesticity to gilded, aristocratic sin was made less easily than it seemed. It was an act of rebellion, and Wilkes was never quite at home in the part of rebel; there was a hankering after quiet, and domesticity, and peace, which

*In 1753 stamp duty was paid on 7,411,757 newspapers; in 1792 on 15,005,760.

was fulfilled in the end, when he settled down to middle age, as an alderman of London, with his daughter, Polly. He lacked the depth and stamina of a true revolutionary. He wanted glamour, publicity, fame; for a short campaign he was magnificent, but he tired quickly. A harsher leader, with greater weight of character, might have focused and drilled the radical resentment of these years into a lasting political force. Wilkes was content with piecemeal victories.

His first was over the question of general warrants. It arose directly out of the change in foreign policy, brought about by the King and Bute. Politically, Wilkes had become associated with Temple and Chatham, and adopted, as it was natural for him to adopt, their attitude to the suggested Peace. Through them he obtained a preview of the King's Speech of 1763, and this he denounced in studied insolence in No. 45 of his journal, the *North Briton*, which already had the reputation for being the most outspoken newspaper of the time.* John Wilkes, although an M.P., was arrested on a general warrant in which he was not named, along with forty-eight other persons implicated in its publication. After he had been lodged in the Tower, his house was ransacked on the order of the Secretaries of State and his papers were removed. Wilkes fought back furiously. Although they had good legal precedents, the government had acted very rashly. In a series of cases Wilkes triumphed against the Crown, and so doing established, not only the illegality of general warrants, but a principle of the utmost importance. The final argument of the Crown had been that they had acted 'of state necessity'. Lord Camden, the judge, refused to accept it, saying 'public policy is not an argument in a court of law'. But Common Law had understood that kind of argument, even in the eighteenth century, although the

---

*Its tone may be judged by this. 'The King is only the first magistrate of this country . . . responsible to his people for the due exercise of the royal functions in the choice of ministers.'

matter had never been duly tried. There had been a steady growth of arbitrary justice in the decisions of the Secretary of State. Wilkes, in the case of general warrants, secured a considerable victory for the liberty of the individual. He also secured an immense political victory. Every action he had taken, he had publicized, using his great flair for advertisement, and every rash or foolish act of the government had been mercilessly pilloried, and distorted as an act of calculated tyranny. Wilkes had become the idol of a savage London, seething with discontent.

But the question of the *North Briton* still remained, even though the government's methods had been condemned. George and his ministers were infuriated with their rebuff and wanted blood. Exerting all the influence they could muster, they managed to get Wilkes deprived of his parliamentary privilege. They also unearthed from his papers an obscene poem, *An Essay on Woman*, which made his defence difficult for his friends. Both Houses of Parliament condemned Wilkes. He was severely wounded in a duel. There was an attempt on his life. His case was scheduled to come before Lord Mansfield, an ardent friend of the government. He was bound to be condemned. He was still extremely popular with the mob, but he had few friends of influence. It was a moment which called for resolution and a sense of mission. But Wilkes went to France for a holiday to recover from his wound. Probably he did not contemplate flight, but, over in Paris, its charms were hard to deny – good food, good wine, brilliant conversations, ardent women. The King's Bench prison was a poor exchange. Wilkes stayed in Paris. He was condemned; he was expelled from Parliament; having failed to return to receive his sentence, he was outlawed. Everyone thought it was the end of Wilkes – even Wilkes.

He dallied for four years abroad, hoping that his friends, once in power, would get him a free pardon. None came. In

1768 there was a general election. Wilkes saw his way out. He returned to England and offered himself as a candidate, first for London, and then Middlesex. He was elected amidst scenes of wild enthusiasm and excitement: his audacity was justified. Worsening relations with America had steadily increased the unpopularity of the government. At first the government proceeded with caution. The outlawry charge was quashed on a technical quibble, but beyond that they were adamant. Wilkes was sentenced to twenty-two months imprisonment and George III regarded his expulsion from Parliament as essential.

Again, the temper of the country, and particularly London, was completely and utterly misjudged, although the presents which deluged Wilkes in prison, the mobs, the placards, the intense public excitement, bordering on hysteria, should have been ample warning. The government, assailed and provoked by methods which bordered on sedition, was undoubtedly acting within its powers, and it is doubtful whether Wilkes and his supporters would have allowed either compromise or conciliation. Yet the government could not have done worse. Wilkesites were killed and their murderers pardoned. And then came the folly of expelling Wilkes from Parliament, time and time again, after each re-election by the Middlesex freeholders, and the final folly of declaring Luttrell, the government candidate, duly elected, although he received only a minority of votes. Legally, the House of Commons was probably within its rights, although it is possible to make out a technical case for Wilkes. The population of London, and of the provincial towns, was not interested in technical niceties. To them the constitution was in danger and there was a threat of tyranny from a Parliament which was unrepresentative and corrupt. To Americans, as well as Englishmen, Wilkes personified Liberty.

Wilkes smarted for revenge, and he needed conflict with

the government to maintain his popularity. After his release from prison, he chose his ground deliberately and well – the reporting of Parliamentary debates. There was again no question that Parliament could suppress reports of its proceedings, but by deliberate provocation Wilkes tricked the government into taking steps which were at first injudicious, and then absurd, and finally dangerous and unconstitutional.* They were denounced vehemently by Chatham, who called their acts 'the acts of a mob not a Parliament'. London was on the verge of open rebellion. Outside its own circles, the government could command neither sympathy nor support. Pride was swallowed and the government retreated amidst cries of derision. The final victory had been with Wilkes.

Wilkes by his actions and by his legal battles had confirmed important liberties, but his influence was more profound than this. He brought Parliament into great disrepute. He demonstrated by his actions its unrepresentative nature; its dependence on the Crown; its corruption and prejudice – facts known for decades, but never so amply demonstrated; nor had the danger to personal liberty, so inherent in such a system, been so clearly proved. And the Wilkes agitation produced new political methods. The public meeting was born and stayed alive. The Supporters of the Bill of Rights Society was founded, the first political society which used modern methods of agitation – paid agents were sent round the country to make speeches, and the Press was deliberately and carefully exploited. Political dissatisfaction was given strength, and coherence, by deliberate organization. Politics were ceasing to be a part of the social life of a gentleman. Organized public opinion had become a factor in politics, and its strength increased, as the government of George III was overwhelmed by problems too vast for its comprehension.

*When they reversed decisions of a court of law.

CHAPTER SEVEN

THE LOSS OF THE AMERICAN COLONIES

I COULD not but reflect on the shame we justly deserve, that a matter of this nature should be so ill attended, a Bill passed a Committee of the whole House that related to the welfare of all the British dominions, and had not fifty members present. (Viscount Perceval, M.P. for Harwich, on the Sugar Bill, 1731.)

Perceval was an Irishman and a philanthropist. As an Irishman he resented the economic bondage, implicit in England's attitude to its overseas possessions. As a philanthropist, actively engaged in founding Georgia, he was thoroughly aware of the immense ignorance, and even vaster indifference, to be found in government circles to all questions relating to the American plantations. Walpole was content to leave American trade to American and London merchants. He instinctively realized that it was too intricate a problem to offer an easy solution. For thirty years Anglo-American relations drifted towards shipwreck. Although the majority of politicians were indifferent to American problems, their minds were quite inflexible on the theoretical relationship between the mother country and her colonies. Colonies were ordained by God to provide raw materials and to accept manufactured articles in return; all trade must be carried in British ships. These were unquestioned articles of mercantilist faith. The majority of the population, however, never thought about America at all; to them it was the dumping ground for thieves, bankrupts, and prostitutes, for which we received tobacco in return.

But America began to announce that it was the victim of

tyranny at the same time that many Englishmen were beginning to develop exactly the same attitude to their own
government. Virginia sent tobacco, and Boston turtles, to
John Wilkes in prison. South Carolina voted him £1,500 to
pay his debts. The Sons of Liberty sent him a formal address
from Boston and Wilkes acknowledged their identity of
interest. Many believed that the fate of Wilkes and America
must stand, or fall, together. Americans and Englishmen
felt themselves to be the victim of the same wanton prejudice,
the same blind insistence on the letter of constitutional
rights, the same ignorance of the broader principles of justice and humanity. And it was to the immense advantage of
America that so many Englishmen were sympathetic to
their struggles. It was even more to their advantage that
American discontent could be used by the Parliamentary
opposition, by Chatham, by Fox, by Rockingham, and by
Burke, to discredit the government.

If England had been ignorant of America and its problems until they became of service in a common struggle,
the same is equally true of Americans. In 1700 the population of the American colonies was 200,000; in 1770 it had
risen to over 2,000,000. Recent immigration had consisted
of German and French Protestants, of Irish peasants and
Scottish crofters, of whores and felons and bankrupts from
London. There could be no loyalty among these immi-
grants, nor was it to be expected among the American born.
Usually their ancestors had left England in resentment and
frequently their ambition had been frustrated by the economically inadequate mercantilist system. There was no
comprehension of the great difficulties facing England;
Americans were concerned with immediate issues and
economic advantages.

The mercantilist system had not worked for a generation,
if it had ever worked at all. It was avoided by smuggling,
by illicit trade with France and Spain, and several American

fortunes had been made by trading with France during the Seven Years War. John Hancock, who signed the Declaration of Independence in large bold letters, so that the King of England might read it without spectacles, had five hundred indictments for smuggling outstanding against him in the courts on the day of his signature. Mercantilism, ineffective as it was, had brought grave economic difficulties to the colonies. The dependence on England for manufactured goods had led to an adverse trade balance, which had created a desperate shortage of bullion, and an inflated paper currency.* English taxation of America was resented partly because it would diminish still further American hard currency. America was experiencing an acute sterling shortage which was hampering its commercial development. It was realized that the freeing of trade with other European countries would rectify this. There were other economic advantages to be gained from independence. The tobacco trade was dominated by London factors and the planters were indebted to the tune of four and a half million pounds, an intolerable and crippling burden, which had been created very largely through the cupidity and dishonesty of the London factors. In many other ways American economic life was frustrated by its dependence on English economy.

In 1763 England had emerged victorious from a protracted struggle with France. The war had been extremely expensive and the national debt had risen from £70m. to £130m. This appalled country gentlemen, who were spending more than fifteen per cent of their income in taxes. Many felt that it was time that others bore their share. The expense of American defence had been very considerable, and Grenville, who followed Bute as Prime Minister, in 1763, was a man who was thoroughly at home devising economies. His policy was simple. Limit the expense and make the Americans pay a share. His method of limiting expense was

*America's adverse trade balance was $9,000,000 in 1760.

to prevent Indian wars. To effect this, he forbade further westward emigration and reserved the prairies for the Indians. Needless to say, the Americans resented his Indian policy and ignored it. The customs system was reorganized, cleared of sinecure holders, and made to work. A serious attempt was begun to suppress smuggling and to enforce the Navigation Acts. Finally, in 1765, a stamp duty was imposed on legal transactions in America; the money raised was to be used towards the cost of colonial defence. Reasonable, sensible, moderate, so Grenville thought. To the Americans it was a final act of tyranny – spontaneously, colony after colony opposed it in violent, almost treasonable, words. It was the beginning of revolution, incoherent, uncertain, inevitable, for the Americans had everything to win, and little to lose, by escaping from a strangling economic servitude.

There was great reluctance on both sides to take the final irrevocable step. At first, England gave way. Wilkes and America were too much for Grenville; he went, and Rockingham, who succeeded him, repealed the Stamp Act, but the threat to authority had been too great to allow it to rest unchallenged. Parliament passed a Declaratory Act, confirming its sovereign right to tax the Colonies. It was the statement of a doctrine, long detested in Ireland, where the phrase 'No taxation without representation' had been used repeatedly for thirty years. Instead of appeasing the quarrel, the government's action intensified it and created intense sympathy for the Americans in all liberal circles. Worse followed. In 1767 Townshend imposed a whole series of import duties, making it absolutely clear that the government intended to raise revenue in America. The colonists' fury was intense, and a pattern of revolutionary organization and leadership began to emerge. Again the British government hesitated; all the Townshend taxes were withdrawn, except the tax on tea, which was maintained for form's sake. The colonists then accused the British government of removing the taxes in order to flood the American market with cheap goods and so ruin the American manufacturers of those goods which had been taxed. This shows how far the quarrel had gone. There could be no final reconciliation; every action which the British government took was inevitably misjudged. When the East India Company reduced the price of tea, so drastically that it was bound to make smuggling unprofitable, the colonies refused to accept the tea and, at Boston, they boarded the ships and threw it into the sea (1773). But before the Boston Tea Party the colonies had been drifting into anarchy and war. The authority of royal officials had been impossible to enforce, and loyalists – Tories, they were called – were actively persecuted. Owing to the forceful expression of pro-American sentiment in England, the government had hesitated to take drastic action. After the Tea Party it took the decision to act with firmness. The custom house was removed from Boston – equivalent to closing the port – and the Massachusetts Charter was suspended. The result was the calling of a Congress in Philadelphia in 1774 and the steady preparation by the colonists for war. But still war did not break out. The end came in April 1775, when General Gage, in Boston, decided to swoop on an illegal gunpowder depot at Concord. Militia tried to stop the British soldiers at Lexington Green; they were overcome, but the British found no powder at Concord. They were harassed and sniped all the way back to Boston. Two hundred and ninety-three British soldiers were killed. War had begun.

It was a war of extraordinary incompetence on both sides; the British decided at once that, if they waited firmly and patiently, the revolution would peter out. The Americans had no money, no trade, no allies, and no army. And they remembered Wolfe's words on the qualities of Americans as fighting men.

The Americans are in general the dirtiest, the most contempt-
ible, cowardly dogs you can conceive. There is no depending on
'em in action. They fall down dead in their own dirt and desert by
battalions, officers and all.

Like most generalizations on national characteristics by
military authorities, it was grotesquely wrong, as General
Gage discovered when he stormed Bunker Hill, outside
Boston. It was an action undertaken to teach the rebels a
lesson. It cost General Gage a third of his troops. Even so,
brave as they were, the rebels had no artillery, no organization, no officers, and at any time in the early years the
British army could have gone wherever it pleased. The same
was true of the navy. The British fleet could have imposed a
total blockade on American ports but, instead, the ships
rode at anchor in New York harbour. It seemed a sensible
enough policy to follow. Positive action would lead to hatred
and a hardening of intention. And all about them British
generals and admirals could see economic chaos and growing
disillusion. But Time proved a fickle ally.

There was plenty of resolve both in Congress and in
George Washington, who had been appointed Commander-
in-Chief. Congress, on 4 July 1776, declared America independent. Washington began his arduous task of turning a
collection of farmers and backwoodsmen into a disciplined
force. At sea, American ships fitted themselves out as priva-
teers and began to prey with devastating effect on British
merchantmen. In Paris Benjamin Franklin secured, not
only French goodwill, but gold to bolster up the ramshackle
American financial system. And the British blundered. A
simple plan was devised to cut the colonies in half. General
Burgoyne was to advance from Montreal to Albany;
General Howe was to move up the Hudson valley from New
York and join him there. No definite orders were given to
Howe. A stately, eighteenth-century army started from Mon-
treal and plunged into the wilderness of the Adirondacks;

it floundered on to Saratoga and there surrendered (1777). Howe, realizing Burgoyne's difficulties, attempted a diversion by capturing Philadelphia and he defeated Washington on the way there. Washington's defeat, however, was totally insignificant beside Burgoyne's surrender, which gave confidence to the rebels. It also convinced the French that the British were in serious trouble. A treaty of alliance was signed with the Americans (1778), and the war became international.

Such a war had long been prophesied. France's losses, even when moderated by George III, had been so great in 1763, that it was inevitable that she should attempt to regain them at the first opportunity. But George and his ministers were intent on a policy of peace and retrenchment; between 1763 and 1775, £6m had been paid off the national debt, but largely at the expense of the armed forces, especially the Navy. In 1779 Spain entered the war against Britain and the combined French and Spanish fleets had the advantage. The command of the sea was lost. The Dutch joined the French. The Northern powers founded the Armed Neutrality, with the intention of resisting the British methods of search. Humiliation and defeat followed; the naval commitments were too much for the depleted British fleet. Although the armies in America were competent and effective, they were hamstrung by a lack of naval support.

The British command in America had decided to reduce the Southern states and, this achieved, to join with British forces under Clinton, which were based on New York, in order to prevent effective aid from being sent from New England to the South. At first the British were successful. The South was reduced, but with a brutality that led to an uncontrollable guerrilla warfare. A first-class French force was landed at Newport which prevented Clinton moving his forces by land to aid Cornwallis, when the situation in the South, owing to the effectiveness of guerrilla resistance, changed. Cornwallis was hemmed in at Yorktown. So long as the British maintained the control of the sea he was safe, but it was lost, and Cornwallis was forced to surrender (1781). It was the end of the war, and Britain's position was almost desperate.

A formidable combination of Indian rulers, backed by the French, seemed to be on the verge of destroying British power in India. The British sugar islands were unprotected. Florida had been lost. The successful defence of Gibraltar did nothing to reassure public opinion, which clamoured for peace. The government of Lord North fell, and peace, on the basis of American independence, was assured. A brilliant victory by Rodney over the combined Franco-Spanish fleets in the West Indies helped to strengthen the British hand in negotiations, which were concluded in 1783, when the Treaty of Versailles was signed.

America gained independence, and America was defined as the land south of the Great Lakes, north of Florida, and westward to the Mississippi. Canada and Nova Scotia remained British; Louisiana was French and Florida Spanish. No one, not even an American, conceived of a United States which stretched from coast to coast. Indeed, everyone was sceptical of the ability of the newborn country to continue to exist. It had no gold, no financial resources, few manufactures; it had no centre of union, no common purpose, but rival state authorities with rival interests. A leading British economist wrote:

They never can be united into one compact empire under any species of government whatever.

George III thought that, after a few years of anarchy, the States would beg to be taken back into the Empire. Few Englishmen believed in their ability to succeed and fewer wished them success. For many, many years Americans were

distrusted and despised as rebels and upstarts who had
nearly ruined the greatest empire of the world since the
Roman.

There is no doubt that the American revolt led to a new
attitude towards the empire. A considerable body of opinion
believed that the colonies were lost through indifference,
through a failure to realize that colonies were like children
who grew to maturity. This analogy had a large appeal. It
gave a sense of moral wisdom, and moral purpose, to economic and strategic conditions, which in their nakedness
would have been incompatible for a nation, which, on increasing draughts of religion and reform, was to become
intoxicated with the idea of its own moral superiority.
American independence was the nation's fall from grace; a
lesson in punishment for sin. For better, or for worse, the
idea of Empire was wedded to a sense of mission.

In its early years the marriage was strengthened by success. Principally it assisted the new attitude which was
developing towards India, the change from trade to government and the idea of trusteeship. India was to influence
deeply British strategy and diplomacy. It led to preoccupation with the Middle East and with Africa. Other circumstances strengthened this new orientation. America lost,
there was nowhere to dump the great accumulation of trans-
portable convicts. James Cook's discovery of Botany Bay
was remembered, and there they went to found Australia,
and to strengthen British interests in the Eastern world.
But, in 1783, at home, the future was foreboding; there had
been a decade of frustration and failure which had brought
the country to the verge of revolutionary action.

CHAPTER EIGHT

RADICALISM AND REFORM
1770–84

A GAMING, robbing, wrangling, railing nation without principles, genius, character, or allies; the overgrown shadow of what it was. (Horace Walpole in 1773.)

All was not well. Each year brought fresh disaster and increased the national debt. From the early sixties there had been a steadily mounting volume of criticism of every aspect of English life. Adam Smith, and his Scottish precursors, maintained that the root of the trouble lay in the organization of England's economy, and the immediate need was to replace mercantilism with free trade. To Jeremy Bentham the trouble was the nature of British institutions, which were built on false principles. The whole administrative machinery, and the entire corpus of legislation, needed drastic reformation on the principle of utility, whose guide was to be the greatest happiness of the greatest number.* Wesley, Whitfield, and their evangelical sympathizers in the Established Church called for a change of heart, for a return to Christian principles and to a Christian life. Opposition politicians believed that George III and his advisers were responsible for the national decay. But the most effective body of men, at least in public propaganda, were the Rational Dissenters, who agreed with Smith, with Bentham, and with Wesley, with Fox and Burke, but limited their horizons and engaged in practical activity. They dominated the first movement for radical reform.

*Adam Smith's *Enquiry into the Wealth of Nations* and Bentham's *Theory of Legislation* were both published in 1776, which also witnessed the introduction of the first comprehensive measure for Parliamentary Reform.

The dissenting academies were the major forcing ground for their brand of political radicalism. These academies arose naturally from the fact that dissenters were not admitted to the universities. Because dissenters were excluded from all branches of civil government, it was natural that they should be more critical of it, and that their interest in the rights and liberties of individual men should be strengthened. They were also freer from the traditional pattern of culture; freer to teach new subjects; and freer to receive new ideas. They were also favoured by chance. In Philip Doddridge, Richard Price, and Joseph Priestley they found teachers and leaders of outstanding intellectual ability and complete integrity of purpose. Their aim was primarily theological, the knowledge of God as manifested in the world, but their approach was strictly intellectual. Understanding could be achieved only through a study of history, philosophy, and the science of politics. The dissenting academies were the first schools in which economics, history, and natural science were systematically taught, and this gave them an attractive modernity, which drew to them pupils from circles far wider than those of dissent. The historical and philosophic approach also gave weight, depth, and a sense of universality to their attitude to politics. Freedom, Liberty, Right, Reason, Necessity, these were the great girders of abstraction upon which they built their treatises of philosophic liberalism. No one doubted their strength to carry the weight of the new hopeful world, which they prognosticated so confidently, which indeed, they believed, was predicted by the course of human history.

On the other hand benevolence, in its widest sense, was absolutely absent from their attitude to life. Liberty and Freedom did not mean liberty to be idle and poor. Poverty, idleness, and crime were to be governed by Reason and Necessity. Poor Laws only cushioned the poor from the impelling force of Necessity and were, therefore, an incitement to idleness. They should be abolished along with alehouses and other distractions. The morals of the poor were to be more effectively controlled and, if need be, slavery should be reintroduced to help suppress crime, for a slave was obviously more useful to society than a corpse. As in Methodism, the virtuous man was to be judged by his social value, by his ability to triumph through strength of will, but the only social services expected from him were his example, and occasional acts of rational charity. Instinctively the poor detested Priestley and, like Guy Fawkes, he was burnt regularly, and, in the end, the Birmingham mob tore down his house.

Amongst the middle classes the popularity of these views of Priestley and of Price was undeniable. In 1776 Richard Price published *On Civil Liberty*: it sold 60,000 copies immediately and double the number in a cheap edition.

Universal as their political philosophy was, the Rational Dissenters were forced to adopt particular political attitudes to specific issues – to Wilkes, to America, to the question of parliamentary reform. Both Price and Priestley were completely pro-American: the success of the colonies was the triumph of virtue over sin; it bore the hallmark of Providence.

In this hour of danger [Price wrote in 1776] it would become us to turn our thoughts to Heaven. This is what our brethren in the Colonies are doing. From one end of North America to the other they are fasting and praying. But what are we doing? – shocking thought. – We are running wild after pleasure and forgetting everything serious and decent in Masquerades. – We are gambling in gaming houses: trafficking in boroughs: perjuring ourselves at elections: and selling ourselves for places – which side is Providence likely to favour?

They were sympathizers of Wilkes, although they hated his morals. They were leaders in the agitation for parliamentary reform, which they based partly on historical and partly on moral grounds. Their historical arguments were

more important, because they helped to foster the strange
national mythology of the Victorians. They believed, as the
Puritans had believed before them, that Saxon England
was the golden age of political democracy. This was destroyed by the Normans and a monarchical tyranny imposed. A long struggle ensued. The first triumph was the
Magna Carta and, since 1215, the democratic and libertarian forces, despite setbacks, had gone from victory to
victory, but final success was jeopardized by the corruption
of George III's government and by the unrepresentative
nature of Parliament. Misleading, yet simple, and it gave
to agitation the comforting sense of siding with manifest
destiny. This was heightened, too, by the course of events.
The stupidity of the government in its battles with Wilkes,
and the handling of the American dispute, made a readjustment in the balance of political power seem more than ever
urgently necessary.

But how was this to be achieved? James Burgh, a pupil of
Price, had, in 1772–3, demanded in his *Political Disquisi-
tions*, which enjoyed enormous popularity, universal male
suffrage, a principle which Wilkes introduced into his
measure for parliamentary reform, rejected by the Commons, in 1776. The same attitude was adopted by another
reformer, Cartwright, in his pamphlet, *Take Your Choice*
(1776), along with the ballot, and annual Parliaments; and
for the next fifty years Cartwright was the advocate of that
extreme political radicalism which was to find its fullest
English expression in Chartism. But even Cartwright believed in Parliament as an institution, whereas Burgh
believed that it might never reform itself, and if it did not,
that it would be necessary to supersede it. Burgh and his
supporters, who were many and influential, learned from
America and from Ireland.* Their project was a Grand
National Association, composed of delegates from County

*See Part III, chapter v.

Associations, formed out of the chief property owners and parliamentary electors. If members of Parliament refused to pledge themselves to the initial, moderate measures of reform advocated by the Associations, the National Association, because it was more truly representative than the Commons, should then act boldly as the Legislature.

As the ministry of Lord North began to crumble under the weight of its own incompetence, this movement, led by Christopher Wyvill and the Yorkshire Association, in preparation for the General Election of 1781, began to take practical steps towards the fulfilment of their aims. There were times, in 1779–80, when revolutionary or, at least, unconstitutional activity against Parliament seemed possible.* In 1780, however, occurred the Gordon Riots, the most savage London riots of the eighteenth century. They arose because Parliament had passed a mild measure of Roman Catholic relief. But, of course, they were also an expression of the deep discontent of the working class in face of the nation's disasters. For days London was at the mob's mercy; destruction was widespread. Prompt action by Wilkes and George III, an incongruous partnership, ended the anarchistic orgy. Although the riots had nothing to do with the Association movement, yet their violence scared the middle classes, and made politicians and political agitators doubtful of the wisdom of embarking on unconstitutional action. Further, the riots played into the hands of those politicians who wished to proceed on more cautious lines than those advocated by the extreme elements of the Association movement.

The disastrous incompetence of the government in dealing with America had, of course, bred discontent within Parliament as well as outside. Also, circumstances were

*The importance of the Association's policy has been clearly demonstrated by Professor Butterfield, to whose illuminating work I am deeply indebted.

peculiarly favourable for an alliance between opposition politicians and public opinion. The natural focus of all eighteenth-century oppositions was the heir to the throne. With the accession of George III, the heir was a child. There could be no rival court to the King's and no prospect of a succession for many years. The opposition leaders were naturally led to a sympathetic interest in the reform movement, which was politically more valuable to them than it might have been. Also, there was quite genuine sympathy for many of the objects of the reform movement. The treatment of the smaller Parliamentary boroughs had become more cynical with the passing of the years, and there was no disguising the fact that they were treated as pieces of negotiable property, advertised as such, and sold as such. Men were conscious that Parliament was losing what dignity and respect it had previously enjoyed, and this, coupled with the national disasters, might lead, it was felt, to a situation of the utmost danger. There were many conflicting views as to what should be done, but the most powerful group was the Rockingham Whigs. Associated with them was Lord Shelburne who, at Bowood, collected around him the Rational Dissenters Price and Priestley and brought them together with Jeremy Bentham. This was the link between the reform movement and parliamentary circles. But the full Bowood House programme was too extreme for most of the Whigs and it added to their instinctive distrust of Shelburne. They were willing to consider reform, but not drastic, revolutionary reform.

They found their prophet, Edmund Burke, Rockingham's own protégé. Burke's views were neither new nor profound, but he gave clear and conscious form to a deeply-rooted, instinctive attitude to politics. The national disasters, he thought, were due to a departure from the traditions established by the Glorious Revolution of 1689. The personal interference in politics by the Crown must cease; the Royal

Household must be reorganized so that the means to corrupt politicians would be destroyed; to regain the purity of elections all Civil servants, no matter how humble, should be disenfranchised. On the other hand, the structure of the constitution should remain, for it was the result of the nation's experience through its centuries of existence. Naturally, to those who enjoyed political power, this was wisdom. And it offered a great deal which was earnestly desired by the rationalists and utilitarians, and it received the support of Shelburne. Throughout the seventies Burke's attitude – the movement for Economical Reform – ran in competition with the Association movement for parliamentary reform and, as the latter went from one public success to another, Burke steadily won converts in Parliament itself, until, in 1780, the Commons in Committee passed the famous resolution, proposed by Dunning:

That the power of the Crown has increased, is increasing, and ought to be diminished.

This, as well as the Gordon Riots, helped to diminish the strength of the Association movement because it was a plain indication that Parliament itself was likely to take action.

In 1782, Lord North's ministry disintegrated; only the personal will and obstinacy of George III had kept it together for so long. The Rockingham Whigs came to power. They made peace with America and they set their house in order. In two measures of Economical Reform the Royal Household was completely reorganized and reformed, revenue officers were disenfranchised, and government contractors debarred from sitting in Parliament. But on the question of the reform of Parliament itself, the government hesitated to take a positive hand, and allowed the Commons a free vote on young William Pitt's motion for an inquiry into the existing system of representation. It was rejected. But even so, it was a victory, and when, after a series of party intrigues, mismanagements, and misalliances, George III entrusted the government to William Pitt, an era of comprehensive reform, economic, constitutional, humanitarian, was confidently expected, for he was the disciple of Adam Smith, the friend of Wilberforce, and the most ardent spokesman for Parliamentary reform in the Commons. In 1784 England seemed to many on the threshold of a new age: for them, there was hope that the country might recover from the bitter humiliations and disasters through which it had just passed. Although they were uneasy and discontented, they longed for a change of heart and a new sense of purpose; and they were convinced that the old ways of life were inadequate to the nation's purpose. But to those who possessed power the future was dark and sombre, they were threatened everywhere; for them, it was a time for tenacity of will, and a closing of the ranks; their world was in danger.

The settled world, the world of Walpole and the Pelhams, had ended. There had been discontent in their world, but the discontented had looked to a past, golden age which prevented them from becoming an organized, disruptive force, for, in politics, the past is always irrecoverably lost and the battle must always be for the future. The English world had grown too large, its interests too complex, its way of life too industrial, for the constitution which a small, leisured, land-owning class had created. The traditional structure of local society was crumbling under the weight of administrative problems of national complexity. But the passing of an age, of a way of life, brought little regret except to the losers. But, in them, it stirred more than regret, it provoked ferocity and a determination to survive with the minimum loss of power. Even so, the tide of economic and social life was running strongly against them. It was diverted not by their own efforts but by the French Revolution and the wars which followed.

PART III

THE AGE OF PITT

*

'Beneath the hills, along the flowery vales,
The generations are prepared; the pangs,
The internal pangs are ready; the dread strife
Of poor humanity's afflicted will,
Struggling in vain with ruthless destiny.'

WORDSWORTH

CHAPTER ONE

THE COURSE OF THE INDUSTRIAL REVOLUTION
1784–1815

WHETHER the population of Britain in the eighteenth century was increasing was a matter for acrimonious debate, which became exceptionally violent between 1770 and 1780. A strong school, led by Richard Price, believed in the decline: this argument was used to explain the weakness of Britain and the decay of her prosperity. But Arthur Young, who had travelled more widely through the length and breadth of England than any other of the controversial-ists, who based their opinions not on observation but on unreliable taxation statistics, denounced the depopulation theory as absurd. He preferred to rely on his senses:

View the navigation, the roads, the harbours, and all other public works. Take notice of the spirit with which manufactures are carried on . . . Move your eye which side you will, you behold nothing but great riches and yet greater resources . . . It is vain to talk of tables of births and lists of houses and windows, as proofs of our loss of people; the flourishing state of our agriculture, our manufactures and commerce, with our general wealth prove the contrary.

However, Young's robust common sense did not settle the issue, and the controversy was prolonged. It was given a new twist, in 1798, by the publication of Malthus' *Essay on the Principle of Population*. This attempted to answer a much greater question than that of the increase, or decline, of Britain's population, but the more sensational aspects of his work were seized on, and distorted, by publicists. Malthusian doctrine was stated to be that increase in population inevitably brought increase in poverty, and that the balance of nature was maintained by natural disasters – war, pestilence, famine. As the book was published at a time of great social distress, these views gained wide currency. Three years later, John Rickman, a friend of Bentham and the Utilitarians, completed and published the first census of the population (1801), undertaken at the order of the House of Commons. For the first time statistics of some accuracy were made available, and the depopulation theory was finally scotched, but the forebodings of the Malthusians were strengthened. The future would bring poverty and social distress. Although misguided and inaccurate, this attitude was an aid to social reform as well as to *laissez faire*. It strengthened the determination of many to try to counter the evils of poverty. That, too, had been the aim of Rickman, who felt that all questions of social improvement must be based on sound vital statistics. The census was a part of the new rational approach to political economy, and it was so successful that the statistical method was rapidly applied to many aspects of English life, so that our knowledge of early nineteenth-century society has a depth and richness of detail which is totally lacking for eighteenth-century England.

The census returns of 1801 and 1811 revealed that the population of England and Wales had increased by one and a quarter millions (9,168,000 to 10,488,000) within ten years, but the most remarkable increase was in the Northern Counties and West Midlands. Great Britain had also become a land of big towns. London, the largest city of the western world, contained over a million people: Manchester with 137,201 was next, closely followed by Glasgow and Edinburgh, both more than 100,000. In England there were eight towns larger than 50,000 but only two, Bristol and Plymouth, were in the South. The change in weight of the population from the South and East to the North and West, faintly discernible from contemporary description in the early years of the eighteenth century, had become an overwhelming fact. This was the result of the growth of industry, which the growth of towns only partially reflected. Towns were still primarily administrative and commercial rather than industrial centres, and of the eleven towns with over 50,000 inhabitants in 1811, six were ports. Sheffield, Birmingham, Leeds, and Halifax had a large industrial population, but it was small compared with the industrial population scattered through the northern countryside, clustered in squalid villages about the mills, which still needed the fast-running Pennine streams for their power.* The same is true of coal and iron and limestone; their presence created village slums, those squalid lines of drab cottages which still run like scabs across the hills and valleys of Wales and the North or erupt like boils on the Midland plain. For decades the industrial revolution was predominantly rural. This had profound social results; it gave rise almost to a new feudalism whose centre was the mill or mine instead of the castle. The workers were dependent on their masters for their houses, their shops, their taverns, their schools, their chapels. It was easy for their masters to discipline the recalcitrant and the complaining, to repress signs of political consciousness and political organization. Without a police force, with its army abroad, Britain survived the intense social distress of the French wars without serious disturbance: the scattered and isolated nature of the depressed classes was the greatest aid to social stability. But the rural nature of industry affected masters as well as men. It gave them a social ideal. As they amassed wealth, they looked with envy and longing at the elegance and authority of the landed gentry. Only if they amassed very vast riches did they sooner or later find

*In 1800 there were only 89 steam engines in Lancashire, Yorkshire, and Cheshire.

their way into the charmed circle of gentility. But, at first, mingling was rare and there was, in consequence, much animosity and hatred on both sides. So long as the squirearchy retained its monopoly of local political power, relations with the new industrial capitalists were bound to be uneasy, and this uneasiness was deepened, because they lived so closely together, and because, in the rural framework of their lives, they were so aware of the difference of their worlds and the conflict of their interests.

The rapid growth of industry in the North was due partly to the more intensive exploitation of the inventions and methods of organization of the middle years of the century, and partly to the incentive of a protracted war, which was felt most sharply in the armament and textile industries. There was no longer any thwarting shortage of labour. The magnificent achievements in urban health of the Improvement Commissioners, together with the development of medicine, and the widespread use of pottery and cotton clothes, had led to a sharp, and steepening, decline in the death rate. Industry had more than it could employ and agriculture more than it could feed. The course of the Industrial Revolution had been retarded by a lack of adequate transport and banking facilities, but these obstacles were largely overcome between 1784 and 1815, or, at least, they became adequate enough to bear the weight of a more rapid industrial expansion. Country banks rose in number from less than 300 to over 700 between 1780 and 1815. But by law joint stock was prohibited, and all banks were privately owned, which led to frequent disasters; even so, they inspired confidence and there was little hoarding. Each bank issued its own paper money and, in provincial England, Bank of England notes were often rare and even regarded with suspicion. However, these banks were as ignorant of the operations of high finance as the London bankers had been in the early days of the century, and the country was flooded with paper money without adequate bullion backing. The strange situation developed of British currency steadily depreciating in terms of foreign exchange, even though she had a large and growing favourable balance of trade. The explanation of why this happened led to a violent controversy between rival theorists of the now fashionable political economy. The outstanding controversialist was David Ricardo, who convinced the public, and finally the government, that the financial stability of a currency depended upon its gold backing. Whether he was right or wrong is still a matter for debate, but what is beyond argument is that cheap money and cheap credit enabled industrialists to take risks, and plan new enterprises, which they could never have contemplated had they depended on their own financial resources.

There is no controversy about the revolution in transport. The canals, the roads, the ships of England were the nation's pride. Inexpensive Irish labour was used to cover Britain with a network of canals. By 1815, 2,600 miles of canal had been built in England; 500 in Scotland and Ireland. They cheapened production and lowered prices. They were the basis of the prosperity of the Potteries which, through the energy and skill of Josiah Wedgwood, captured the world's china trade. But the revolution in road transport was more vivid, more exciting, to contemporaries. Road engineering did not begin to improve until the last quarter of the century, and it was given a strong stimulus, in 1784, with the introduction of the mail coach for the rapid transport of letters and passengers. The stage coaches responded to the threat of competition and road surfaces were improved to help faster travel. In 1754 it took four and a half days to travel from London to Manchester; in 1788 the journey had been reduced to 28 hours. The expense was great. It cost Sir Walter Scott £50 to travel from

Edinburgh to London. The improvement in road communication did nothing to cheapen production or widen
markets. Its vital contribution was that the roads acted as
nerves between the nation's economic brain in London and
its muscles in Wales, in the Midlands, and in the North. A
more closely integrated commercial and industrial society
was the result.

Equally important, but more spectacular, was the growth
and improvement in ports and shipping. By 1810 the tonnage
of ships using British ports, excluding Irish and coastwise
trade, reached 2 million tons, and to accommodate it 30 acres
of new docks – the first adventure in iron architecture – had
been built in London between 1800 and 1810, during the
course of the most desperate war Britain had yet fought.
These docks made London the greatest port in the world.
But the Thames was more than a port, it was also a vast
shipyard in which nine-tenths of the East Indiamen were
built, and refitted, in the great yards of Blackwall and
Rotherhithe. Bristol, Liverpool, and Glasgow were like
London in miniature, but the whole coast of Britain was
studded with towns, villages, and hamlets which depended
upon ships, and the sea, for their livelihood. Men were
conscious that the nation's wealth and power depended
upon their mastery at sea, the pride of their ancient
tradition.

But both the roads and the ships at sea were poised on the
verge of a profound revolution. In 1801 Lord Dundas
travelled along a Scottish canal in a small steamboat. Ten
years later steamboats were engaged in regular passenger
travel on the Thames and Clyde estuaries, and one of them
made the journey from Glasgow to London. For centuries
railways, rollers, and inclined planes had been used to get
coal from the mine to the waterside, but between 1800 and
1815 the application of railways became much wider than
this. Tracks of over twenty miles were laid down and active

and successful experiment in the application of steam loco-
motion for driving wagons had taken place by the time
George Stephenson patented his first engine (1815). But as
yet these were signs and portents, which only the most per-
ceptive could understand; for the common man the wonders
of his world lay in the canals which climbed the Pennines,
the flying coaches between London and the North, and the
China clippers which covered the 15,000 miles from Canton
to the Channel in 109 days. It was a revolution of which he
was conscious, for it took place very largely in the space of
thirty or forty years, within the lifetime of thousands of
men, underlining in a vivid and spectacular way that theirs
was a new world, and strengthening their beliefs in the pro-
gressive nature of human destiny, which were to achieve the
force of a religious conviction.

The industrial basis of this wealth was the steady spread
of the technological advances and the improved methods
of industrial organization of the sixties and seventies. This
was most obvious in the rapid development of the cotton
industry in Lancashire, where the factory system and power-
driven machinery were most commonly found, but, even
in Lancashire, pockets of old-fashioned industrial methods
still lingered side by side with the new. Big mills and the
great textile magnates, the Fieldens, the Peels, the Horrocks,
were, of course, exceptional. For one capitalist of this
stature, there were fifty small masters, men risen from the
ranks of the workers themselves, or yeomen with a little
capital, lured to Manchester and the boom towns by the
prospect of quick wealth. The same is true of the light metal
industries of Birmingham, of Sheffield cutlers, and the small-
scale potters of the Five Towns. But the great fortunes were
made by those industrialists who adopted most completely
the new methods, and this was obvious to contemporaries.
In consequence, the little men struggling for their fortunes
detested the ancient legislative restrictions, especially the

long, seven-year apprenticeship, and they became ardent supporters of radicalism, which offered them a world of *laissez faire* in which employment and wages were to be allowed to find their own levels by the law of supply and demand. The exploitation of the workers was usually most intensive in the smaller factories where the desire to accumulate capital was most feverish.

The increased wealth of England which these developments brought was not widely diffused. There were more families of middling wealth than ever before, but the vast bulk of the population fell within the contemporary category of 'labouring poor'. It is difficult to judge whether their lot grew better or worse with the intensification of the industrial revolution. It varied according to the trade, to the district, to the employer, and to the nature and temperament of individual men. But the poorest working men today would have found the lives of their ancestors almost unbearable. The hours of work were fourteen, fifteen, or even sixteen a day, six days a week throughout the year except for Christmas Day and Good Friday. That was the ideal time-table of the industrialists. It was rarely achieved, for the human animal broke down under the burden; and he squandered his time in palliatives – drink, lechery, bloodsports. Or he revolted, burned down the factory, or broke up the machinery, in a pointless, frenzied, industrial *jacquerie*. The worst of these outbursts occurred in the Midlands and the North, in 1811 and 1812, and they were dubbed Luddite Riots, after their leader, Ned Ludd. But riots on a smaller scale were endemic in the industrial areas.

The prolonged war with France made social conditions worse. The naval war, which ultimately involved the whole of Europe, distracted the flow of overseas trade, causing intermittent and violent industrial depressions. Before the war Britain could more or less feed its population, except in bad years; by the end of the Napoleonic wars Britain could feed its increased population adequately only in bumper years. The result was a general, if fluctuating, rise in the price of food. The situation was aggravated by the reckless financial policy of the government, which created an unnecessarily heavy drain on the nation's gold resources, which led ultimately to the financial crisis in 1797 with the suspension of cash payments. Although the inflationary trend was partially checked, prices had been driven up. The consequences were years of high prices and low wages, intermingled with years of high prices and high wages. The workers in industries which depended on the export trade suffered most, and those in industries directly associated with the war, coarse textiles and armaments, suffered least. By and large, the industrial poor did less badly than the rural poor, and some economic historians have been at considerable pains to show that there was a slight improvement in the purchasing power of their wages during the Napoleonic wars. Be that as it may, the condition of life for the poor was extremely wretched. It was impossible for most of them to live a life of more than bare subsistence and the natural disasters of their personal lives – unemployment, sickness, death of the breadwinner – left families in utter destitution, for the State had little conception of social service; its only answer for unemployment and poverty was the workhouse.

*

Throughout this period the pace of the agrarian revolution was intensified. With a rapidly growing population, the demand for basic foodstuffs – wheat and meat – increased yearly. The corn laws secured a protected market for the farmer in the years of abundance. During the long wars with France the years of scarcity made his profits even higher, for, willing as the government was to obtain grain from any source, it was impossible to secure enough to reduce the inflated price of scarce corn. The demand of the armed forces, especially for meat, was a further stimulus to agrarian prosperity. It is not surprising that the large, fat, rubicund, pugnacious figure of John Bull, which graced the patriotic prints and cartoons, should always be depicted as a farmer. The wealth to be made from farming, and the narrow margin of safety in British food supplies, led naturally to a keener interest in the improved techniques for agriculture. Over two million acres of land which had been neglected since the high middle ages, if it had ever been cultivated at all, were enclosed and brought into cultivation between 1790 and 1810. Very considerable experience was gained in farming difficult land, in the use of fertilizers, and in the mixture of soils. Great impetus to the 'New Agriculture' was given by the formation of the Board of Agriculture in 1793. This curious body had no bureaucratic function or authority. It was a body composed of enthusiasts for the new agriculture – Lord Lonsdale, the Duke of Bedford, Coke of Holkham, Sir John Sinclair, and Arthur Young – and it was supported partly by public funds and partly by private subscription. Its function was to popularize new methods in draining, in horse-hoeing husbandry, in the use of fertilizers, and in sound crop rotation. It pressed vigorously for the adoption of new agricultural machinery – especially the threshing machine and the new type of wheeled plough. It was responsible for Erasmus Darwin's *Phytologia* and Davy's *Lectures on Vegetable Chemistry*. It campaigned for General Enclosure Acts and simpler legal machinery. It organized a thorough, critical survey, county by county, of the agricultural resources and development of Britain. Productivity and profit were increased. But new machines, draining, and fertilizers required capital; so did the risk of cultivating bad land. The larger the farm, the easier it was to take considered risks. The large farm, too, made profits more certain for the greatly increased capital investment which the new methods required. Medium-sized farms of 300 acres, and large farms of 500, became common in the better cultivated counties, and the very small farms of twenty or thirty acres tended to disappear.

Of course, these changes affected the structure of rural society. They encouraged the growth of large estates and gave the aristocracy wealth which few of the new industrialists could rival. This prosperity was shared by the tenant farmers, fewer in number, but greater in local and political importance, than hitherto. They did not make great fortunes, but estates of £10,000–£12,000 were very common for a successful farmer, which was sufficient to cut him off sharply from the lower grades of rural society, and to give him an identity of social and political interest with the landlords, and with those professional classes, attorneys, solicitors, surveyors, and land agents, who battened on problems arising from the ownership of land. The gulf between this rural middle class and the agricultural labourers widened decade by decade. The growth of farms and the increased use of machinery lessened the demand for labour. Cottage industry which, in many counties, had been associated with rural life, especially spinning, was rapidly disappearing: the cottage was poorer. With enclosure vanished common rights, and small holdings, and the labourer's plot was reduced to a cottage garden. Wages, although they rose, lagged behind the soaring price of food. Rural poverty was far worse, and more widespread, than urban poverty, and it was intensified by the Speenhamland system, introduced in Berkshire in 1795, which put a premium on pauperism. Discontent was directed with savage violence towards the new machinery and new methods. At times, as in Cambridgeshire, the revolt of the rural poor was so intense that the army had to be used to suppress them. The poor drained away to the towns, to the boom towns of the North, or to London with its insatiable demand for domestic servants.

But not enough left the land. Rural poverty and destitution, with the heavy charge on the parish which they created, was a nightmare for local administrators and social reformers. Great publicity was given to the question of poverty by the publication of Eden's *The State of the Poor* in 1797,* and by the trenchant denunciations of William Cobbett in his *Political Register*, founded in 1802. Everyone realized that the old Law of Settlement, by which relief could be claimed only in the parish of one's birth, was outworn, but there was little agreement as to what to put in its place. In any case only a handful of men felt that the problem was capable of solution; the vast unimaginative majority regarded poverty as an inexorable law of nature.

Social distress and poverty, widespread and intense, had existed throughout the century in both town and countryside. As the years passed the incidence of poverty changed according to social and economic developments, but it changed in little else. In 1800, as in 1700, hours were intolerably long, wages low, houses insanitary, and hunger commonplace, but there was one improvement: because of a deepening knowledge of medicine, and because of a growth of social discipline and organization, the poor stayed alive in increasing quantities, feeding the factories and the towns, the living material which created the wealth of England.

*Pitt gave his secretary, Cumming, his copy to read. Cumming made a parody on the index.

CHAPTER TWO

THE RECEPTION OF THE FRENCH REVOLUTION

Apart from the Industrial Revolution, there was no profounder influence than the French Revolution in moulding the course of English history in the eighteenth century, and the development of its political expression in the nineteenth. Before 1789 English middle-class radicalism had been ignorant of the strength of the social forces which, from time to time, it aroused for its own purposes. At the time of Walpole the Corporation of the City of London had purposefully, and deliberately, inflamed the lower classes against the authority of the government; at the time of Wilkes there had been no hesitation in using the economic grievances of journeymen for political ends. Radicals were familiar with the philosophic arguments about liberty and the rights of men, and they were experts in corruption and institutional decay, but they were profoundly ignorant of the social consequences of a constitution overturned by violence with the aid of the lower classes. They had no idea of the potential force of their political conceptions and organizations. The French Revolution left no one in doubt as to the strength of the middle and lower classes, and their capacity to achieve political dictatorship by violent and revolutionary methods.

In England some politicians had toyed with a radical attitude according to the exigencies of factional politics; others were enthusiasts for the purification of the institutions of government; there were a few, largely outside formal politics, who were anxious to achieve a new definition of political power and willing, if necessary, to take extra-constitutional steps to achieve it. In the radical agitation associated with Wilkes, and in that which occurred towards the end of the American war, these groups had worked together in an unholy alliance. Their great achievement had been the Economic Reforms of Burke; their greatest failure the collapse of the Bill for Parliamentary Reform, introduced, but not pressed, by William Pitt in 1785. The French Revolution made the continuation of such an alliance impossible, for it made all radicals define their attitude to it and, by implication, to revolutionary methods for achieving political ends. From 1789 there is a deepening division in the ranks of English radicalism: a left wing, composed largely of working men with middle class leaders; a right wing of young Whigs devoted to the cause of parliamentary reform and the person of Fox. Both groups were viewed with distaste by the erstwhile reformer – Burke. For him the revolution in France was a European catastrophe, dynamic but evil. His denunciation of revolutionary change was published in his *Reflections on the Revolution in France* (1790), which was immensely successful in Tory, as well as in some Whig, circles, for it clarified in lucid language the fears and suspicions long felt towards radicalism by those with a large share in the ancient order of things. Burke, too, pleaded for a vigorous policy of opposition to France and to the use of force by England and her allies to repress the revolutionary movement. Year after year he returned to his charge, stirring up hatred against radicals and reformers. Loyal societies sprang up throughout the provinces to counter the activities of the rapidly increasing radical clubs.

In some ways Burke himself was largely responsible for the growth of these radical clubs. Thomas Paine, an active and violent supporter of American Independence, had replied to Burke's *Reflections* in his *Rights of Man*, in which he had proclaimed the necessity for universal suffrage and the sovereignty of the people. He denounced monarchy and aristocracy as useless archaisms. His book was immensely popular. It was welcomed by the Society of Constitutional Information, formed in 1780 by earlier radicals to further the cause of Parliamentary Reform; and in 1792 almost every town in England and Scotland had a club for Constitutional Information or its Society of Friends of the People. Most of their members were drawn from the working or lower middle class, with a sprinkling of educated, professional men. The general aims of these societies seem to have been twofold: to spread Paine's idea by reading his works, and to impress the government with the strength of the public opinion favourable to France. At the same time they kept up an adulatory correspondence with the National Assembly in France and with various Jacobin clubs. This movement was given a closer organization by the formation of the London Corresponding Society, which, under the energetic leadership of Thomas Hardy, a working man, acted as leader for the provincial societies. Two general Conventions were held at Edinburgh and at the second, in 1793, the British Convention of the Delegates of the People, a number of emergency resolutions were passed which provided for secret leadership and meetings in case the government took repressive action. A revolutionary organization was in the making and the government took steps to thwart it.

From 1790 the government had viewed this growth of lower-class radicalism with increasing alarm. It was strongest in the big industrial towns of the North and Scotland, towns where, owing to the primitive police organization, it was almost impossible to keep law and order. And, although most of their political aims were in appearance mild enough, such as the support of the Duke of Richmond's plan for parliamentary reform, the tone and language were the tone and language of revolutionary France, and that was enough to create an atmosphere of panic. In October 1790 the Habeas Corpus Act was suspended, and again in 1794, when the government was really frightened by the British Convention, radical leaders were arrested. In England, Hardy, Horne Tooke, and others were acquitted on a charge of high treason, but in Scotland others were found guilty of sedition and given savage sentences of transportation. Mass agitations and mass meetings went on and so alarmed the government that Pitt secured the passage of new and more stringent Treason and Sedition Acts in 1795 and in 1799. Corresponding Societies were forcibly suppressed. Finally, in 1799, with the harsh laws against Combination, the government killed two birds with one stone. These Acts made the combination of workmen in clubs and societies, for the sake of improved working conditions and wages, conspiracy. It enabled manufacturers to keep down wages in spite of the rising price of food. At the same time the government was enabled to eradicate one of the best breeding grounds for subversive propaganda. Time and time again these Acts were invoked to suppress savagely and indiscriminately the movement towards trade unionism.

The Combination Acts caused no comment in political circles. It was a general conviction that the working man was a savage, unprincipled brute who naturally thirsted to overturn a society so obviously not to his advantage. In fact, it was so obviously not to his advantage that many men of goodwill were troubled in their consciences and impelled to good works. They longed for a sober, diligent, enlightened, and, above all, Christian working class who would understand that suffering and poverty were in the nature of things but not inimical to man's salvation. This attitude towards society and the individual, which was implicit in Methodism, spread in Anglican circles and enlightened influential men, giving rise to a new evangelism. Its civil leader was William Wilberforce, its religious, Simeon: each had a cluster of devoted adherents, Simeon at Cambridge, and Wilberforce at Clapham. The Clapham Sect was the more influential because it consisted largely of Members of Parliament. Apart from their general evangelism, which they regarded as the ultimate solution of social antipathy or social distress, there was also agitation for more specific types of social reform or missionary enterprise.

Their greatest and most successful crusade was for the abolition of the slave trade. Before 1772 Negroes were commonly bought and sold in England. This is a typical advertisement taken from the *Liverpool Chronicle* of 15 December 1768:

TO BE SOLD,
A FINE NEGROE BOY,
Of about 4 Feet 5 Inches high.
Of a sober, tractable, humane Disposition, Eleven or
Twelve Years of Age, talks English very well, and
can Dress Hair in a tollerable way.

There were about ten thousand slaves in England, when Lord Mansfield made his famous judgement in Somerset's case (1772), by which slavery was declared illegal in this country. The care of freed slaves led the Clapham Sect into a demand for the suppression of the trade, and also into colonial experiments, for they were responsible for the foundation of Freetown, Sierra Leone, as they thought it desirable to return the freed slaves to Africa. The experiment was not a success, but it did give rise to an increased interest in Africa and its exploration. The constant agitation by the Sect in Parliament was more successful: the trade was abolished in 1806.

The success of the slave trade agitation has obscured a great deal of the Sect's other social work. Active Christianity was the panacea for the world's ills; in consequence, education and missionary enterprise were more important to the Sect than the more direct ameliorations of social conditions, such as control of child labour, shorter working hours, cheap food, and higher wages. They and their supporters set up schools for the poor, especially Sunday Schools for ragged children, which were interested principally in the inculcation of morals and Christian principles, as narrowly interpreted by Simeon or Wilberforce. Not only the poor received their attention, but also the wealthy and middle classes, and, in spite of much aggressive opposition, prudish piety began slowly to replace that frank cynicism which had been the hall-mark of eighteenth-century fashion.

Although the vast majority of the natural leaders of English society detested the principles of the French Revolution and their frightening manifestations in industrial England, there were a few who felt that by modest compromise the danger to their country could be averted. These were principally young Whig aristocrats, led by Charles James Fox. They had a genuine belief in reform, but reform also offered them definite political advantages. The French Revolution and the French wars had greatly strengthened Pitt's hold on political life, and many Whigs felt that the power of the new Toryism could be broken only by the widening of the franchise and the representation of the industrial towns. But they would have nothing to do with Paine's principles or Thomas Hardy's organization. Conscious of the dangers of fanning the political aspirations of the lower classes, they restricted their activity to parliamentary agitation.

The appeal of the French Revolution, however, was much deeper than that for Charles James Fox. Fox was a man of immense personal stature, witty, eloquent; all his attitudes were heartfelt and generous, instinctive with sympathy for the dispossessed. Although he disapproved of many of the acts of the revolutionaries, their insistent demand for liberty made him forgive them readily. At the expense of his own popularity and the strength of his party, he pressed constantly for peace with France. Although these views tended to isolate him in political circles, he became the idol of those intellectual bohemians who supported the French Revolution.

In literary and artistic circles, and in the wilder-living sections of the aristocracy, the Revolution was at first immensely popular. It seemed to mark the end of that medieval obscurantism in institutions and beliefs associated with the *ancien régime*. It symbolized the destruction of despots in Church and State, and the chance of an era in which human personality, freed from the shackles of the past, could achieve a new fulfilment. Restraint was hypocritical and dangerous – dangerous because it thwarted natural expression. There had been plenty of licence and promiscuity in English literary and aristocratic circles before Rousseau and the Revolution became popular, but it had been free from insistent self-justification; nor had the pose been fashionable that licence and promiscuity were a part of a higher morality. A dangerous mutual antipathy grew up between conventional society and a large section of the English intellectual and literary world. The principles of the Rights of Man were no less detestable when expressed in poetry or used as a guide to life.

Raffish, extravagant, unpatriotic men, such as Godwin, Shelley, and Byron, played into the hands of the evangelicals who viewed artistic expression and intellectual inquiry with distrust. It was the beginning of the tradition that society was antipathetic to the true artist; that he was forced to live above the conventions and beliefs of ordinary men.

To the fashionable world, the Revolution brought an edge to pleasure and a nagging fear. The influx of émigré aristocrats made the English peerage more conscious of what it had to lose and more inclined to make brave and extravagant gestures to Fate. Corinthians, Macaronis, Brighton, and Brummell, the uneasy half-fantasy world which the Prince Regent built about himself, were defensive expressions against a growing apprehension that time was short.

In both the fashionable and literary worlds there was a necessity for cliques to preserve courage, and to promote admiration and respect in a hostile world. Need for ostentation was dangerous to taste. The danger was increased by the irresponsible vulgarity of the Prince Regent. Both were more harmful because of the narrowness of the world within which they operated. Again, the fulminations of the evangelicals against luxurious living were given fresh justification and the demand for middle class piety was strengthened. Plain living in ugliness acquired moral virtue.

In spite of the divergent effects of the French Revolution on English society, its major influence was to strengthen the Englishman's sense of tradition. It gave a strongly conservative bias in religion and politics to the middle class, although they accepted much more of the philosophic dogma of the Revolution than they were aware. It also made crystal clear two necessities for a stable State—sound administration and the ability to compromise in a changing world. To have fought for so long, and so frequently alone, against half Europe, and the force and vigour of revolutionary peoples and ideas, naturally increased the Englishman's pride, especially so as it had been done without loss of wealth, without economic or social exhaustion. It naturally led to an assumption of arrogance towards the rest of mankind and to the growth of an intense moral vanity.

CHAPTER THREE

ART AND SCIENCE
1784–1815

THERE were many indications that the urbane, classical attitude to literature with its insistence on form and manner and restraint had ceased to appeal to the majority of the reading public long before Wordsworth and Coleridge published the *Lyrical Ballads* in 1798. Fiction, because it appealed to a wide, less cultured, and less intellectual public, had escaped the narrower restraints and more formal attitudes of poetry. Defoe, Fielding, Sterne, Smollett, and even Richardson had a warm response to the deepest human experiences. They had an eye for the colour and movement of life, for its pathos, ribaldry, and fun. They were vigorous and exuberant, if formally sensitive and platitudinously moral for the sake of their female readers. They had little or nothing in common with Pope, Swift, or even Cowper and Gray. But they were forerunners. They do not mark in any way the beginning of a great school of English novelists, for none of them really believed in the novel as an art capable of expressing the deepest experience of man. They wrote to make money, to entertain, or to preach a simple morality. Poetry still retained its place as the supreme vehicle for literary achievement and remained the citadel of the classical attitude. The walls were undermined and crumbling and they turned to dust at the first blast of the trumpet of avowed romanticism.

William Blake's *Songs of Innocence* (1789) and his *Songs of Experience* (1794), as well as Burns' poetry in Scotland, had been conceived in direct, simple language which could be understood by anyone who could read. But Wordsworth and

Coleridge proclaimed the necessity to write in such a way; they made a conscious endeavour to break with the past, to give poetry a new and wider appeal. Like almost all literary theories, it led to silliness and absurdity and excess: to the simple-wittedness of Peter Bell. But the revolt had a deeper purpose than a change in literary style and form. It was a return to the language of Milton and Shakespeare, to the language of the heart. Poetry had lost its sharp edge, its lyricism, its sense of man's tragedy and despair: too sensitive to absurdity, it had taken refuge in form and manner. About absurdity the Romantics did not care, they seem to have been indifferent to it. Without this indifference they could not have poured forth as much poetry as they did. Nothing blights the creative spirit so much as fear of a solecism. The achievement of Wordsworth and Coleridge, and the early work of Byron and Shelley, made this one of the greatest epochs of English poetry. Essentially it was the poetry of early manhood, with an aching sense of childhood lost; full of wonder, and awe, and pity, a mixture of wild aspiration, confidence, and despair. In nature they found a solace which gave stability and purpose to the chaos of feeling.

Of course, such an attitude has many dangers. It leads easily to false attitudes, to posing, to self-conscious eccentricity, to spurious nonsense. The revolt against the immediate past led to a cultivation of the art and culture of the Middle Ages, or rather, of what the romantic revivalists enthusiastically believed to be gothic and medieval. And in this direction the romantic movement is seen at its worst. But, utterly bogus as it was, it did some incidental good. There was a revived interest in Chaucer, in Langland, in the relics of English medieval poetry, architecture, and art to offset the pornographic lucubrations of Monk Lewis and his followers. The greatest harm which this deliberate cult of medievalism did was that it began to undermine the confidence of the fashionable world in its own taste. A decay of the classical and palladian forms in architecture and decoration became inevitable, and contemporaneous with the lovely buildings with which Nash adorned London was the monstrous horror of Fonthill Abbey, the herald of Victorian Gothic. There is no clearer indication of the wavering nature of taste, of its desperate insecurity, than the Regent's Pavilion at Brighton. The decline in painting was far less rapid. At first, indeed, painting gained tremendously from the development of the romantic attitude, especially landscape painting. In the hands of such great painters as Turner and Constable a sense of wonder and awe suffuses their pictures as it does the poetry of Wordsworth and Shelley. The same spirit gave added grace and quality to those painters of great distinction who made this the greatest age of English landscape paintings. The old classical attitude was mellowed with a romantic vision but they held it sufficiently in check. Only in the genre painting of Morland, Wilkie, and Mulready was there any hint of the future's desperate collapse of taste.

Nevertheless, the revolt against the aristocratic and classical attitude to life was very profound, and it is seen most clearly in the development of a self-conscious intellectual bohemianism which deliberately set out to live in defiance of accepted moral codes. Men and women had lived in sin frequently enough in the eighteenth century, but they had felt no compulsion to justify their acts on the highest ethical principles. The intellectual bohemians, Godwin, Shelley, Mary Wollstonecraft and their circle, sinned for the sake of revolt rather than for enjoyment, and then justified themselves by the principles of liberal philosophy. Squalid as their lives were, they had important consequences for English literary tradition. The golden age of romanticism became associated with wild living and antisocial behaviour, and contributed to the growth of the myth that the true artist was incapable of living in society.

Nothing was more fallacious, for the works of all the great romantics had a wide appeal to the cultured middle classes. They were written in the language which they could understand, about the common themes of human life – love, childhood, death, man's relation with nature. And it is the poetry which deals with these themes which has become a part of the English tradition, rather than the bitter railings against society of Byron and Shelley.

The cultured middle class swallowed greedily all that it was offered – tales of mystery and horror, Miss Edgeworth's moralizings, Scott's long narrative poems, journals of travel and adventure, Miss Austen's novels, and an endless stream of historical works. The appetite was insatiable, but, to keep it appeased, there was an increased output of books, journals, and newspapers. The *Edinburgh* and *Quarterly* reviews, with their violent, self-confident attitude and their unrelenting antagonism, enabled thousands to enjoy all the excitement of a literary war. *The Times* and the *Morning Post* with their frank and bitter comments on the conduct of government sharpened the political criticism of the well-to-do. For the less affluent, there were the homely diatribes of William Cobbett in his *Political Register*, and the cheap volumes of the *Novelists' Magazine* and *British Classics*. There was an intense intellectual ferment, a sense that there were vast seas of knowledge to be charted. Uninhibited by the growth of professional standards, every science and every art was an open invitation to the amateur.

The spread of knowledge and the development of scientific curiosity had been greatly accelerated by the rapid expansion of publishing, the foundation of circulating libraries, and the growth of Literary and Philosophic Societies. Circulating libraries at fashionable spas were an old-established institution, but it was only towards the end of the century that the great provincial towns obtained subscription libraries, containing thousands of books covering the whole range of human knowledge. Another expression of the same thirst for knowledge and culture was the growth of Literary and Philosophic Societies on the model of Manchester's, founded in 1781. By 1815 every provincial town of importance had its society, supported by both the local aristocracy and the local manufacturers, who were equally aware of the social value of scientific discovery. Davy, Dalton, Stephenson, three great figures of scientific invention, were all trained in their provincial societies: Davy at Bristol, Dalton at Manchester, and Stephenson at Newcastle. No other aspect of English cultural life had such whole-hearted middle class support, because the intention was completely and avowedly utilitarian – the search for useful knowledge which would maintain England's industrial supremacy. The same support was forthcoming for the encyclopedias and journals which helped to disseminate the knowledge gained.

Between 1771 and 1815, there were four editions of the *Encyclopaedia Britannica*, the last of twenty large volumes: and each edition enjoyed an enormous sale. But more important than the encyclopedias were the journals. For over a century the Royal Society had published its *Transactions*, but they were slow to appear, and consisted of finished work, and they did not make for quick communication of the essential developments of work in progress. To meet this need Nicholson began to publish his *Journal of Natural Philosophy, Chemistry, and other Arts* in 1797, and it played a part very similar to that played by *Nature* today, and was a vitally important factor in the acceleration of scientific discovery. Equally helpful was the development of specialized journals and specialized societies which were the natural development of rapidly increasing scientific knowledge and of its increased popularity. By 1815 the Linnean, Geological, Zoological, Horticultural, and Astronomical Societies, and many others, had been founded. They were viewed with some suspicion by the Royal Society and its dictatorial

President, Sir Joseph Banks, who felt that its supremacy in science was being undermined. But the spirit of the age was against authoritarian monopolies, and there were too many ardent amateurs of science, drawn from all classes of society, who wanted to meet, to discuss, to experiment, and to publish. The range and width of interest in science is clearly demonstrated in two societies which met in London. In 1800 the Royal Institution was founded, and it drew support from the wealthiest aristocrat circles of England – Bedford, Devonshire, Egremont, Spencer, Holland, Palmerston, Winchilsea, etc. At the same time, a group of East End apprentices, of whom Michael Faraday was one, was meeting and experimenting in the laboratory of William Allen, a philanthropic chemical manufacturer.

The results of this activity were vast and valuable. The flora and fauna of Britain, the nature of its soils and rocks, were examined in detail, catalogued, and given a rough scientific order and arrangement. Some of the work was haphazard and jejune; most of it had to be done again and very soon; but it provided the intellectual justification for that rational and historical approach to nature which found its genius in Charles Darwin. And, of course, there were particular and detailed discoveries of exceptional scientific value. The greatest advances were made in chemistry. Thomas Young and Sir David Brewster, however, did fundamental work in optics, a subject which had been considered closed since the days of Newton. But, in chemistry, the two great names were those of Sir Humphrey Davy and John Dalton. Dalton was a slipshod experimentalist who lived from hand to mouth, teaching and lecturing in Manchester and the North. But he had a restless original mind, not easily satisfied by the conventional framework of chemistry, and by 1804 he had established the atomic theory. Others – Thomson, Wollaston, Berzelius, and Gay-Lussac – refined and confirmed his hypotheses; both the chemical notation and the chemical equation, the essential basis of all modern chemistry, had been evolved by 1815.

Sir Humphry Davy's life was a vivid contrast to Dalton's; it was a story of a romantic rise from poverty to fame, riches, and respectability, dear to the heart of the Victorian moralists who exaggerated Davy's contributions to science and gilded his character. The son of a poor Cornish Methodist, Davy obtained his first scientific training under the eccentric Dr Beddoes who ran the Pneumatic Society at Bristol. He was noticed by Count Rumford, the founder of the Royal Institution, who brought him to London as a lecturer. At that time the scientific world in London was preoccupied with the voltaic battery which Sir Joseph Banks had introduced in 1800. Knowledge of the intimate relations between electricity and chemistry was rapidly acquired, and, more important, rapidly diffused through the new scientific journals. In 1806 Davy made a clear, accurate, and final statement of the relationship which, although it was based primarily on the experimental work of other men, gave him the foremost position in British science. Using electrical methods, Davy made a series of experiments which resulted in the discovery of sodium, potassium, magnesium, and many other metals and – what was at the time more important for the textile industries – of chlorine, which was used for rapid bleaching. Almost all of Davy's discoveries had the same obvious, practical value for an alert industrial society: his safety lamp for miners (1815), and his work on agricultural chemistry (1813), added immensely, and in a similar way, to his public fame. No scientist since Newton had so captured the nation's imagination: first a knighthood, then a baronetcy, with wealth to support them, were the inevitable rewards. And yet Davy's genius is admittedly not of the first rank. He was singularly fortunate in his time, and he was exceptionally shrewd in his appraisal of other men's work.

Yet Davy at the Royal Institution was something of a portent, the clear, practical demonstration of the value of 'useful knowledge' to an industrial society. The desire to acquire knowledge, for which his life was such an encouragement, ran both wide and deep in English society. It is hard now to recapture the intensity of belief and faith that the accumulation of knowledge and practical scientific understanding would bring both to the nation and to the individual, wealth, success, and happiness. Mechanics in their Institutes, and the nobility at the Royal Institution, were moved by the same urgent sense of intellectual discovery, by a common feeling that they stood on the threshold of a new world which, unaided, man's mind could compass. In these years science was woven into the fabric of the nation's life.

CHAPTER FOUR

THE BRITISH IN INDIA

THE greatest public sensation of the 1780s was the impeachment of Warren Hastings, the result of political intrigue and personal vendetta. Nevertheless, the trial raised the whole problem of imperial relations and human morality, which could no longer be ignored, for in the second half of the eighteenth century the position of the British in India had changed profoundly. In the days of Pitt's grandfather, Thomas Pitt, Governor of Madras, there were fewer than fifteen hundred English in the whole of India, including wives, children, soldiers, and seamen waiting for their ships. This tiny population was confined to Madras, Calcutta, Surat, and Bombay, where they lived a close corporate life, living together in their factory, and dining together at their common table with the Governor presiding and the ensign at the bottom to act as toaster, officer, carver, and chaplain. Trade, and trade only, was their business, and there was a genuine self-interested attempt to make themselves agreeable to the Indians. They adopted Indian habits in food and dress, and frequently married Indian women, sending their children back to England, or keeping them in India, according to the lightness of their skin. They showed deep respect for Indian authority, and an intelligent curiosity about the customs and habits so alien to their own, but, throughout their relationship with the native population, there was a refreshing absence of moral vanity. They were traders, proud of their race, determined to make money as fast as they could, but they were wholly free from the sense that manifest destiny had called them to rule the native people.

The condition of India presented a vast temptation. In 1707, Aurangzeb, aged 88, the last great Mogul Emperor, had died: for a generation his sons and daughters fought to inherit his Empire. This gave a splendid opportunity for the Mahratta powers, whom Aurangzeb had been unable to crush, to terrorize North and Central India. It also enabled the Imperial Governors of Bengal and Southern India to create for themselves what were, in effect, independent kingdoms, paying only lip-service to the titular Emperor at Delhi. And as the years passed, temptation to exploit this anomaly became allied with fear that others might. During the latter part of the seventeenth century the French had become firmly established at Pondicherry and Chandernagore, rival ports to Madras and Calcutta. And it was a Frenchman who showed the British the way to power and to profits undreamed of by their merchant brothers. In 1746 Britain and France were at war. Dupleix, the Governor of Pondicherry, realized that the Imperial authority at Delhi was no longer effective in the Carnatic. He flouted the Nawab's orders not to attack Madras, ousted him with ease, and captured the place. The Treaty of Aix-la-Chapelle in 1748 gave Madras back to the British. But Dupleix refused to return to the *status quo*: he had discovered the way to power and he meant to follow it. In 1749 a palace revolution gave him his opportunity; the French candidate for Nawab, supported by French arms, easily succeeded. The French were paid enormous sums for their services and granted large territories. Such lavish success whetted Dupleix's appetite; he aimed at control of Central India and the expulsion of the British, but his mistake was to put control before expulsion. His divided forces enabled the British to reorganize and to discover Robert Clive. Clive had a suicide's temperament, careless of life yet of infinite endurance so long as death was near. In 1751 the defeat of the French puppet at Arcot gave the British the Carnatic. Clive

collected a fortune and returned to England in triumph in
1754, the same year which saw Dupleix recalled by France
in disgrace.

The same year, too, witnessed the disembarkation of the
first royal troops in India, for previously the only British
armed forces had belonged to the Company. The continued presence of a British army in India was subtly to
change the British way of life and the British attitude to the
natives. In 1754, however, their presence was considered
temporary, until Franco-British rivalry was resolved, for,
although the British dominated the Carnatic, the French
controlled Hyderabad, and the British position in Bengal
was rapidly deteriorating. The Nawab of Bengal had
watched the manoeuvres in the Carnatic with growing distress, and finally he decided to throw the British out of Bengal before they threw him. He seized Calcutta, but failed
to follow up his advantage, and allowed Clive to land with
effective reinforcements. The victory of Plassey followed
(1757). Clive had a puppet ready to succeed the defeated
Nawab. He then charged the new Nawab £200,000 for his
services and the freehold rights of 900 square miles around
Calcutta for the Company. The prize money for the rest of
Clive's lieutenants and the Company's servants was in the
same generous proportions. Both the Carnatic and Bengal
were virtually British and, although the French continued
to fight, their position in India was hopeless.

But these successes of Clive were more momentous for
the British than the French. There was an army in India of
far greater strength and efficiency than any native army.
Clive had demonstrated how colossal fortunes could be
raised by its use. It was a way of getting rich which made
mere trading seem humdrum and petty. Interference in
native politics did not stop with placing a British puppet on
the throne of Bengal: within a few years the East India Company was administering the taxes and justice of Bengal –

at an immense profit. India became an El Dorado for young men in search of a fortune, and the Directors of the East India Company discovered that they wielded a patronage of royal dimensions. It is true that there was a high risk of death, but, if the young writer or ensign survived, he could expect to return to England within three years with a fortune sufficient to set himself up as a country gentleman. If he were a man of ability, he might reasonably expect to rise high in the Company's service, and then return with a fortune equal to a peer's. This wealth, displayed with the ostentation natural to an eighteenth-century gentleman, excited intense envy. It was not long before envy allied itself with morality. By what right had these nabobs to extort such riches from the simple peasantry of India? The Commons brought themselves to investigate Clive's actions, but they were satisfied with his outburst:

By God, Mr Chairman, at this moment I stand amazed at my own moderation.

For the East India Company knew how to bait its hooks. Writerships and commissions flowed to the relatives of politicians in power. The East India Company retained its monopoly, although it ceased to trade, and royal troops were kept in India to defend its rights. They were not kept in idleness. Until the utter defeat of France in the Napoleonic wars there was constant intrigue by the French, in the hope that they might recover their lost empire, with any native power that showed an aggressive attitude to the British (of these the most important were the Mahrattas and Hyder Ali in Mysore). The Mahrattas had long dominated, terrorized, and pillaged Central and Northern India and they hated to see their prey disappear into the British maw. Hyder Ali was an exceptionally capable buccaneer who hoped to secure a kingdom for himself by astute power politics. With the French drilling and officering these native forces the British position was frequently precarious, especially so during the disasters of the American war of Independence.

It was due entirely to Warren Hastings that the situation was saved at all. Hastings was out to win, but he had three wars to fight at once – war with British enemies, war with his allies eager to desert, war with his own council. He had little time, even had he possessed the temperament, to stop and consider the consequences of his actions, and his actions were often brutally sharp. When he was impeached they were subject to minute examination, and to fervid denunciation by the greatest orators of the age, but it was natural that he should be acquitted, for every action he took was designed to make British rule paramount in India. It was easy to show that the administration of Bengal, reformed by Hastings, was both more efficient and more just, if no less expensive, than the native rule which had preceded it. But the impeachment of Warren Hastings raised issues far deeper than the specific charges of cruelty and extortion for which he was tried. Clive had become an empire builder by accident. Hastings was an empire builder by design. His policy was to build up a strong British India, to extend its territories, when opportunity arose, and to knit to this paramount power independent Indian princes by offering them military protection against their enemies. It was a policy of war and Imperial expansion. It involved immense political and administrative responsibility, and could be carried out only at an immense cost, which ten years of Hastings' governorship showed the Company could not afford. To Burke and the Whigs such a policy was utterly wrong on grounds both of morality and expediency. It was morally wrong to inflict ourselves, unbidden, on the Indians and it was absurd to allow a Company, designed for commerce, to wield imperial power, but the prospects of Empire were too attractive and it was comparatively easy to counter the moral arguments of Burke by the assumption that the British were divinely ordained to rule the Indians for their own good.

It was a long struggle. It took twenty-four years to defeat the Mahrattas and Hyder Ali, and later his son, Tipu. But when it was at last accomplished, under the great governorships of Cornwallis and Wellesley, the whole sub-continent was in Britain's control and vast areas were directly under her administration. Such a fundamental change of policy required a drastic alteration in the machinery of government of British India, but this was forthcoming. The Regulating Act of Lord North in 1773, and the India Act of Pitt in 1784, modified the Company's powers and instituted a system of Dual Control which was to last until 1858. According to Lord Curzon:

Had a Committee been assembled from the padded chambers of Bedlam, they could hardly have devised anything more extravagant in its madness or more mischievous in its operation.

The Company floundered in hopeless difficulties. The host of civil servants and soldiers which it employed were indifferent to the Company's profits; they were interested only in salaries and incidental perquisites. In consequence, the Company staggered on the verge of bankruptcy, borrowing larger and larger sums from the government. Relief of a sort was obtained from the development of the opium trade with China.* The Company possessed a monopoly on all opium grown in Bengal. It was smuggled into China in return for silver. The profits were so great that, by 1815, Chinese bullion was one of the major supports of British administration in Bengal. The necessity

*This was due to the foresight of Warren Hastings. He realized that, owing to its disastrous effect on the peasantry, it was a short-sighted policy to allow Indian consumption and he insisted on its export to China.

of these transactions was not debated. The end justified
the means: without the China trade there was a danger
of the whole British rule in India collapsing, and the collapse of British rule would mean a return to anarchy and
civil war.

The end justified the means: the end also had to justify
the increasing moral arrogance of the British Raj. This
developed rapidly as soon as the British acquired political
power. In earlier days, and even in the days of Clive and
Hastings, Englishmen had mixed in a free social intercourse with the natives, learnt their language, and appreciated native culture.* That attitude withered and died
rapidly during the Governor-Generalships of Cornwallis and
Wellesley. Cornwallis excluded all natives from the higher
posts in government service and discontinued the honours
customarily paid to Indian nobles. Wellesley carried the
process further and excluded all Indians and Eurasians
from the regular entertainment at Government House.
Such an attitude came even more naturally to the canton-
ments, for a successful army usually despises its victims,
while exiled wives of army officers were intent on preserving
their insular standards and, by the assumption of social
arrogance, attempted to dispel the fear aroused by the alien
and incalculable environment. The more English society in
India isolated itself from native life, the more bigoted
became its attitude. This bigotry was encouraged by the
growing evangelism amongst the English middle classes,
for the missionaries and chaplains who flocked to India at
the end of the century were horrified by many native
customs which they made no attempt to understand. The
attitude of moral righteousness was again strengthened, for
obviously a race wallowing in such abominable heathenism

*T. G. P. Spear, *The Nabobs*, a work of profound understanding of
Anglo-Indian relationship in the eighteenth century, to which this
chapter is greatly indebted.

was unfit to rule.* Distasteful as it was for the Englishman to
live in India, the provision of good government was an
obligation which he could not avoid. It was his destiny.
This attitude pervades the letters and memoirs of Anglo-
Indian society in the early years of the nineteenth century;
the boisterous selfishness of 'Diamond' Pitt and the calculated greed of Clive are long past. There was better government, greater security of persons and property, than India
had known for a century. Ignorant as it was of native ways
and native customs, the British Raj was more just, and less
extortionate, than its native counterpart. But the spiritual
price India had to pay for these improvements was intolerably heavy, and one of the minor miracles of history is that
the Indian Mutiny did not happen sooner and with greater
effect.

*'The Hindoo appears a being nearly limited to mere animal func-
tions and even in them indifferent. Their proficiency and skill in the
several lines of occupation to which they are restricted, are little more
than the dexterity which any animal with similar conformation but with
no higher intellect than a dog, an elephant, or a monkey, might be sup-
posed to be capable of attaining. It is enough to see this in order to have
full conviction that such a people can at no period have been more
advanced in civil policy.' Lord Hastings, 1813, quoted by Spear, *op. cit.*
p. 201.

CHAPTER FIVE

THE IRISH EMPIRE

THROUGHOUT the eighteenth century trade to Ireland was the most important branch of English overseas trade. Three-quarters of Irish land belonged to Englishmen or to Anglo-Irish Protestant families. By the middle of the century three-quarters of a million pounds in rent was leaving Ireland each year for the pockets of the absentee landlords living in England. No wool was allowed to be exported except to England; its manufacture was absolutely forbidden. Irish ships were not allowed to trade with the colonies, although economically Ireland was extremely dependent on America.* In consequence, Irish economy was forced into a course which was fatal to a fast-growing peasant population. The raising of sheep for wool, and of cattle for beef, whose free export to Europe was permitted, led to the growth of vast grazing grounds and consequent depopulation. The peasantry was driven to find a precarious subsistence on a potato patch, frequently no larger than a garden. Famine was endemic. What little prosperity Ireland enjoyed was derived from the linen manufactures which England was unable to make for itself, but this hardly touched the vast majority of the peasantry, who lived in want and in fear of starvation. Thousands shipped themselves to the plantations on terms little better than slavery, which were preferable to the slow starvation at home. Even so, there would have been far greater disasters than the famine of 1730, or 1741, had it not been for the rapid development of potato cultivation. The potato kept the Irish alive and allowed them to multiply. The population, despite famine and emigration, rose from

*Flax seed and potash for bleaching linen came from America.

two to four millions, but it was a population living in a squalid poverty unparalleled in Europe.

It is manifest [wrote Swift in 1727] that whatever stranger took such a journey (through Ireland) would be apt to think himself travelling in Lapland or Iceland, rather than in a country so favoured by nature as ours, both in fruitfulness of soil and temperature of climate. The miserable dress, and diet, and dwelling of the people; the general desolation in most parts of the kingdom; the old seats of the nobility and gentry all in ruins and no new ones in their stead; the families of farmers who pay great rents living in filth and nastiness upon buttermilk and potatoes, without a shoe or stocking to their feet, or a house so convenient as an English hogsty to receive them – these may, indeed, be comfortable sights to an English spectator who comes for a short time to learn the language, and returns back to his own country, whither he finds all our wealth transmitted.

It is bitter but true that the English were responsible. They had invaded Ireland, conquered it, and, in spite of repeated rebellion, mastered it. Each rebellion had been followed by harsh retribution. The land had been taken away to compensate the victims and to pay for the alien administration which the conquerors had imported. Its economy had been rigidly and absolutely subordinated to England's. Whatever the causes, each rebellion appeared as a Roman Catholic revolt against a Protestant government, so every pacification brought harsher laws against Catholic priests or Catholic laymen, who were deprived of the few rights of citizenship which eighteenth-century governments accorded to their people. In consequence, the institutions of government in Ireland were all in the hands of a small Protestant minority. The Church consisted of fat, profitable bishoprics, a few good benefices, and hundreds of parishes which were so poor that frequently a dozen held in plurality were insufficient to support a curate who dunned his wretched parishioners for a tithe of their potato harvest.

Even so, practically no preferment went to an Irishman. Walpole and Newcastle, desperately short of patronage, made sure, through Archbishop Boulter, that the Irish Church helped to appease the clamour for place. The Irish Parliament was as alien as the Church. It had few powers; all legislation was controlled by the Privy Council in London, and the only effective right which it possessed was to tax the country. Its boroughs were rotten by English standards; elections scarcely took place – in the reign of George II the same parliament sat for thirty-three years. No Catholics, of course, were allowed to hold a seat. The atmosphere of farce clung to the administration. The Viceroy spent only one-fifth of his time in Ireland, but this was far longer than most of his senior officials, who drew incomes of £2,000 to £9,000 a year to support their leisure in England.

The Irish were browbeaten, plundered, and despised, but it must be remembered that they were a defeated race, and the memory of their rebellions was keen in the minds of Englishmen both within Ireland and without. They clung obstinately to an alien religion whose superstitions and ritual were regarded with abhorrence by both Anglican and Deist. The country swarmed with brigands, and destructive outbursts of agrarian discontent indicated their natural propensity for revolt. Irish prosperity and Irish freedom might be a serious threat to the liberties, happiness, and growing wealth of England. A Protestant Church and State, closely supervised by London, and an economy strictly subordinated to England's, seemed to offer the only solution to the Irish problem which had troubled England for centuries.

For a time it worked: 1714–60 is a period of relative calm in Anglo-Irish relations. The ancient Irish nobility was either defeated and dispersed through its Jacobite loyalties or full of a desire to please in order to retain what it still held in Ireland. The Elizabethan, Cromwellian, and Williamite aristocracies had been too recently scared by the

support accorded to James and too fearful of Jacobite intrigue to develop an independent attitude to Whitehall:
many of them, gorged with recent plunder, were buying their
way into the English aristocracy.

But the years passed. The Fifteen and the Forty-five hardly
stirred the Irish calm. Yet the calm was deceptive. The years
of peace had allowed a culture to develop which gave to
those who owned and ruled Ireland, Protestant and Catholic alike, a sense of common destiny, akin almost to national
consciousness. Many of the Irish nobility could afford to live
and to build in a way which they felt necessary to their
social standing only if they lived and built in Ireland: the
extravagance of English aristocratic living was beyond their
means. Dublin became a real capital with buildings of
beauty and magnificence, a social setting for the leaders of
Irish opinion. Those leaders of opinion were not perturbed
by the atmosphere of patronage and influence, nor by the
unrepresentative nature of Irish institutions, but they grew
to dislike, and to hate, their alien nature. Although they
were called Reformers, they did not wish to reform Irish
institutions; they wished to free Irish economy from foreign
control and to win legislative independence.*

As England floundered from disaster to disaster in her
relations with America, clouds gathered over Ireland.
Hating Whig oligarchy in all its forms, George III's government had broken its hold on Irish institutions in 1767, only
to drive a powerful section of Irish Protestant opinion into
opposition. From 1767 to 1775 the Irish government survived
only by doubling the civil and pension lists and, even so, a
proposal to tax absentee landlords ten per cent nearly
became law, defeated only by North's personal intervention.
In 1775 Henry Grattan and his friend and patron, the Earl of
Charlemont, took charge of the reform movement. Grattan
was a superb orator who had studied Chatham's style with

*Cf. Maurice James Craig, *The Volunteer Earl*. Cresset Press, 1948.

professional understanding, to his own great benefit. But Grattan was also a great politician, capable of exploiting the complex opportunities created by the American war.

The modest prosperity which Ireland enjoyed was seriously endangered by the loss of American markets; the failure of American exports of flax seed and potash ruined the linen trade; the lack of potato flour made the threat of famine more certain and more ominous. The militia was withdrawn for American service and Ireland was wide open to invasion from France. Grattan and Charlemont organized the United Volunteers. The Volunteers proclaimed their absolute loyalty to George III and their irrevocable decision to secure economic equality and an independent legislature for Ireland. Eighty thousand men were organized, drilled, and armed. At war with half Europe, defeated in America, the helpless British government could only concede, at first piecemeal and then wholesale. In 1780 trade, especially to the colonies, was partially freed; dissenters were relieved of their disabilities, and even a modest measure of relief was given to the Catholics. This infused confidence into the Volunteers, who demanded full legislative independence. By 1783 the British government had reluctantly given way: Poynings' Law, which had controlled Anglo-Irish relations since the reign of Henry VII, was swept away and the Act of Renunciation declared 'the exclusive right of the Parliament and courts of Ireland in matters of legislation and judicature'.

And yet no true solution had been achieved. Although the Legislature was independent, it was venal. The Executive remained English, appointed and dominated by London. Grattan realized that the Irish Parliament must be reformed if a solution was ever to be found for Ireland's gravest problems – the problems of religious liberty, of absentee landlords, of a depressed peasantry, and a dependent commerce. Otherwise each measure of reform could be defeated by the political pressure exerted by the administration on an unrepresentative Parliament. Ample demonstration of this was rapidly forthcoming.

In 1785 Pitt, the apostle of free trade, decided to complete, more or less, the economic freedom of Ireland, and to make the British Isles a single fiscal unit. Apart from a few reservations, trade between the two islands and with the rest of the Empire was to be without restriction, and in return for the privilege Ireland was to pay half a million a year to the upkeep of the navy. These propositions rapidly passed the Irish Parliament, but the English House of Commons would not tolerate them. They were amended almost out of existence and a compliant Irish executive resubmitted them to its legislature, only to have them spurned. As ever in the face of defeat, Pitt withdrew his interest and ignored the implied difficulties. Ireland was allowed to drift to disaster.

An independent legislature and loyalty to the Crown had failed to solve the fundamental difficulties which faced Ireland. To all Irishmen of spirit, Presbyterian and Catholic, the alternative was plain. With America in revolt and the Volunteers in arms, Whitehall had capitulated before Irish demands. The wars with revolutionary France provided another golden opportunity for Ireland to force its demands by an implied or overt act of rebellion. The United Irishmen were formed by Wolfe Tone and reluctantly the threat was recognized, but again the English capitulation was half-hearted. The Catholic vote was conceded, but Catholics were denied membership of the Irish Lords or Commons. The United Irishmen entered into an alliance with France and made a bid for independence. The situation was exacerbated by the Viceroy, Fitzwilliam, exceeding his powers and promising full Catholic emancipation. When he was recalled in 1795 the bitterness was intense. The country was swept into disorder. The Protestants, fearful of full emancipation, especially in Ulster, reorganized the

Orange Society and harried the Catholics. The United Irishmen plotted with the French and attempted to organize resistance. Between 1796 and 1798 they were overborne and broken up with extreme brutality; complete licence was given the troops to torture and to kill, to drive home a bloody lesson on the Irish. Maddened by these excesses, and hopeful of help from France, the Catholics rose in 1798. The French were thwarted and the rebels cut to pieces at Vinegar Hill.*

England maintained its supremacy, but at a bitter price; the old tradition of brutality, destruction, and massacre, had been reforged. For a brief moment in the eighties it had seemed that Grattan and Charlemont would conjure forth a new Ireland, independent, urbane, an amalgam of Protestant and Catholic, Gaelic and Saxon civilizations. The moment had been illusory – a mirage which blotted out the hard realities of economic and administrative subordination.

Pitt well realized the necessity for an attempt at a new solution, but he was willing for the lesson to be driven home. As he waited for the destruction to create the exhausted mood for compliance, he evolved a new policy. Legislative independence had failed, commercial independence was not acceptable to English interests, full independence was strategically unthinkable. Against these failures and impossibilities could be placed the century old success of the Union with Scotland. Pitt decided to pursue the same policy: to create a legislative union in return for religious toleration. The corrupt Irish Parliament was bribed into acquiescence. The Act of Union became law. The Irish Parliament was swallowed by the British. But Pitt failed to persuade George III to the necessity of emancipation, and he resigned. But, with or without emancipation, it was a solution which totally ignored the realities of the Irish situation, and one which could lead only to fresh frustration, bitterness, and strife.

*Cf. chapter seven.

CHAPTER SIX

WILLIAM PITT AND THE NATIONAL REVIVAL

THE political world in the eighteenth century was exceptionally stable and enduring, once a pyramid of interest had been built up by the King's ministers. But there were times when the pyramid was in ruins, and then the political world experienced an instability which no modern State could endure. Once a political system had been broken up, either by the change of monarch or by the pressure of external events, then family groups coalesced about their chosen leader and jockeyed for the control of the administration which would give them the opportunity to create a permanent majority in Parliament. In these times of instability old political enmities were quickly forgotten and political creeds adopted, or abandoned, with an ease which, at times, embarrassed even contemporaries. It was usually the politician with little sense of politics who was the most quixotic; but men such as Walpole, Pelham, and Pitt, the creators of enduring systems, maintained a resolute and consistent purpose.

The collapse of Lord North's administration in 1782 began a period of extreme instability which lasted until the emergence of William Pitt from the successful general election of 1784. Lord North and his numerous supporters were in discredit: the Whigs were split into two hostile groups – the Rockingham Whigs and the Chathamite Whigs, led by Shelburne. There was the King who disliked intensely the old Whig families and the Prince of Wales who distrusted the Tories. There were also a number of influential groups with special interests – nabobs, West Indian merchants, slavery abolitionists, and parliamentary reformers – who were willing to adjust their loyalties. Political calculations and political intrigue were endless, but the methods by which Pitt emerged as the victor demonstrate with exceptional clarity the nature of eighteenth-century politics.

In the struggle which lasted for two years there were four men of quite exceptional ability and distinction – Charles James Fox, the Earl of Shelburne, afterwards Marquis of Lansdowne, Edmund Burke, and William Pitt. Fox was the leader of the young Whig bloods who gambled away their patrimony at Brooks'. He was witty, generous-hearted, and the most brilliant speaker in the Commons. He was a loyal friend of the Prince of Wales and expected to become his Prime Minister when George III died, or became permanently demented, a contingency upon which he gambled away most of his political credit. But he was a formidably able politician, popular in London, and the leader of a devoted group in the Commons. Shelburne was a far abler man, the friend of Bentham, Priestley, and Price; he maintained a shadow administration at his country palace, Bowood, which kept him better informed on all questions, financial or diplomatic, than any minister in power. Yet he had no capacity for leadership. He was known to his contemporaries as 'Malagrida' or 'the Jesuit': no one would trust him and in the matey world of politics he was shunned and avoided. Edmund Burke had neither the birth nor the wealth for the leadership of a political party. He was the servant philosopher of the Rockingham Whigs, by his speeches and writings giving his party a universal significance as the one true representative of great Whig principles. But his attempt to lift the Rockingham Whigs to political conceptions above faction was consistently betrayed by the practical ineptitude of his colleagues, and in the end he was driven to alliance with Pitt. William Pitt, the younger son of Chatham, had less capacity but more character than Fox,

Shelburne, or Burke. He was deeply and consistently ambitious: but his aim was to rule, and his sense of politics was equal to his resolution.

With the fall of North, the Rockingham Whigs took office, but in alliance with the Chathamites. Fox and Shelburne were Secretaries of State, Burke was Paymaster-General; Pitt refrained from taking minor office on the ground that it would be incommensurate with his dignity and abilities. While Burke purged the Royal Household with his Economical Reform Bills, Fox and Shelburne opened the preliminaries for peace with America and her allies, and steadily intrigued against each move the other made. Rockingham died, and George III saw an opportunity of ridding himself of Fox, whom he hated. The King sent for Shelburne and asked him to form a ministry. Fox, of course, resigned and went into opposition. Shelburne offered Pitt the Chancellorship of the Exchequer; he was twenty-two and he considered the office important enough to accept. Fox was furious. He detested Shelburne and he was bent on revenge. With Fox and his followers in opposition and with Lord North and his followers in opposition, too, the Shelburne administration was exceptionally insecure. Shelburne sent Pitt to try to win over Fox. The interview was short.

'It is impossible for me to belong to any administration of which Lord Shelburne is the head.' This declaration of Fox was, no doubt, meant as an invitation to treachery. 'Then we need discuss the matter no further. I did not come here to betray Lord Shelburne.' This was Pitt's lofty and confident reply, which immensely impressed the narrow world of politics. It had the advantage of driving Fox into a more desperate opposition. He entered into formal coalition with Lord North, the man whom for twelve years he had denounced, with all the bitterness and sarcasm of which he was the master, as the sole cause of the disasters of the American wars. He threw aside all consistency for immediate political advantage. Against the combined numbers of Fox and North, Shelburne was doomed. George III, distracted at the necessity of sending for his bitterest enemies, begged Pitt to form a ministry. Pitt refused. He considered the time inopportune. He was waiting for Fox's folly to mature.

It was not long to wait. From the very start of the ministry of Fox and North, whom the King had been forced to accept, there were defections from Fox's ranks, by politicians astute enough to realize that an uneasy alliance of discredited Whig and discredited Tory could never survive against the implacable hostility of the Crown. Fox's only hope of success was to flatter those powerful pressure groups – the City, the nabobs, the reformers – with whose support he might have maintained a precarious hold on office. Pitt's attention to these groups was assiduous in the extreme. At this time Wilberforce was his closest friend and he maintained all of his father's City connexions. Instead of placating, Fox alienated, once more by a political manoeuvre which was too obviously cunning, and too obviously in his own interests. The East India Company exercised a vast patronage,* and it was admitted to be in need of reform. The control of the East India Company's patronage would help to cancel the patronage difficulties caused by the royal disapproval. Fox introduced his India Bill (1783) which transferred the Company's affairs to Commissioners, appointed by the Government, which meant, of course, by Fox himself. It was the end of Fox. The City was thoroughly alienated. Although the Bill passed the Commons, George III personally intervened in the Lords, and it was thrown out. For Pitt the time was ripe; he became Prime Minister. He was twenty-four years old, and, apart from one short break, he remained Prime Minister for the rest of his life.

His rise to power was a feat of astonishing brilliance and acumen. He had brought powerful and divers political

*Cf. chapter IV.

forces to associate his name with their hopes or fears. For
the King, he meant release from servitude to Fox and North;
for the City, the right to enjoy and dispose their own patronage; for the reformers, the fulfilment of their hopes; all
these were in an agony of suspense until they were certain
of his survival. Pitt knew it to be a question of time. Before
he could risk a general election, it was necessary that the
Treasury should complete a thorough investigation of electoral pressures, enticements, and punishments – the only
sure way to secure a parliamentary majority. Again, in
order to tempt connexions to support him, Pitt had to
demonstrate his capacity to survive; and that he knew lay
in his resolve and his royal favour. He ignored defeat after
defeat in the Commons and ennobled his followers. Fox
scoffed and blustered, but his majority steadily fell, and he
failed to carry out his threat to stop supplies. When Fox's
majority was reduced to one, Pitt, secure in the electoral
calculations of the Treasury Solicitor, dissolved Parliament.
The general election was bitter and expensive, and, although the Treasury Solicitor's calculations were inaccurate in some of their details, the general result was, as he
had forecast, a *majority*. In the popular constituencies Pitt's
association with Wilberforce had proved invaluable. But his
greatest asset was the political inconsistency of Fox, who
was thoroughly distrusted, both for his alliance with North
and for the oligarchical implications of his India Bill. The
happy coincidence of popular approval and Treasury intentions, rare in eighteenth-century politics, gave Pitt a greater
majority than he anticipated and made the election of 1784
the marvel of the age.

Pitt's path was still beset with difficulty. Apart from the
Grevilles, he was connected with few great families and, in
Wilberforce and his reformers, he possessed allies whom the
King regarded with absolute disfavour. Pitt had little diffi-
culty with the reformers. In 1785 he introduced a measure

of parliamentary reform which included provision to re-compense borough patrons to the tune of one million pounds for the loss of their property. The measure was defeated and Pitt's conscience cleared. In 1787, and again in 1791 and 1792, Pitt spoke eloquently on behalf of the abolition of the slave trade, but he accepted the negative decision of the House with tranquillity. For Wilberforce and his reformers, he did the minimum commensurate with political safety and political honour. For his major support he had to look elsewhere – to the King and to the City of London; the only two institutions which could in any way counterbalance the opposition of the territorial magnates.

With the King's help, he recreated the House of Lords, swamping the old Whig aristocracy under a deluge of new titles; at the same time, old orders of Knighthood – Garter and Bath – were greatly enlarged, and a new one – St Patrick – created so that the loyal should not go empty away to fall under the temptation of opposition. Many of these honours went to the *nouveaux riches*, to men of great wealth, connected with the City, upon whose support Pitt increasingly relied. No minister worked harder to secure them. In his first year of office, he piloted safely through the Commons an India Bill which regulated the affairs of the East India Company with the minimum disturbance of the Directors' interests and patronage compatible with easing, if not appeasing, public opinion. In his great budgets from 1784 to 1787 Pitt set about reorganizing the finances of the country. No change had taken place since Walpole had turned his back on reform after the rejection of his Excise Scheme. Pitt had read Adam Smith and had become a devoted disciple: his aims were to free trade from restraint, and to encourage trade with Europe to offset the loss of the American colonies. At the same time he had to restore public confidence in the country's finances. The American war had been paid for in a hand-to-mouth fashion in loans: the result was a chaos similar to that which faced Walpole after the wars of the Spanish Succession.

It is upon his solution of these problems that Pitt's reputation, as one of the greatest peace ministers, rests. He simplified customs and reduced them drastically on consumption goods, especially tea, in order to check the ravages to the financial system caused by smuggling. Whenever he could, he abolished any measure which tended to check the flow of raw materials to British manufacturers or which impeded the export of finished articles. Devoted to the principles of free trade, he tried in 1785 to extricate Irish manufacture from its subservience to British interests. But Irish plunder was too valuable to risk for a theory's sake and the Commons refused to go with Pitt. He accepted the rebuff with the lofty unconcern which so maddened his enemies. He then proceeded to negotiate a commercial treaty with France (1786) based on those same principles of free trade. With finance he was less successful. Attracted as ever by the theoretical approach, he accepted the views of Dr Price on the National Debt and Sinking Fund. But Dr Price's view was based on a fallacy and, apart from an immediate gain in confidence, Pitt's operations with the Sinking Fund produced no benefits. Nevertheless, as the years passed his reforms in the national economy and the lavish honours royalty bestowed created for Pitt an unassailably strong position; before Fox and his Whigs stretched the wilderness.

The position was dramatically changed in November 1787 when, in Windsor Great Park, the King descended from his carriage and addressed an oak tree as the King of Prussia. A demented King called for a Regency, but the Prince of Wales was the bosom friend of Fox and his Whigs. Pitt prevaricated. He demanded a Committee to search for precedents, when everyone knew there were none. He proposed limitations on the Regent's powers. Fox and his supporters threw Whig theory to the winds and talked of the

Prince assuming his inherited rights without more ado. Pitt hinted at a possible recovery, and found a physician to support him, but at the same time he prepared to go back to the bar. The Whigs drew up their ministry, and jus' as they were prepared to take office, the King showed unmistakable signs of recovery. By March 1788 Pitt was back in power, bleakly weeding from his ministry all who had been willing to compromise with Fox for the sake of office. And Fox, with his unconstitutional and unwhiggish declamations, was discredited more deeply than ever.

Nor was Fox's position improved when next year he acclaimed the fall of the Bastille and the revolution in France. Burke, his greatest ally and the devoted friend of a lifetime, deserted him and joined Pitt. Others followed Burke. A few friends, principally Grey and Sheridan, remained loyal, pressed for parliamentary reform, railed at Pitt and the corruption of the age, drank toasts to the Revolution but ostentatiously displayed their patriotism by joining the militia. It was a policy difficult for men of influence to understand and harder for them to follow. More and more Pitt seemed the sounder man, the true guardian of political tradition. The way in which he quietly dropped reform, the steadiness of his distrust of the French revolutionaries, his stern attitude to homespun radicals, compelled their admiration. More than ever did the appellations Whig and Tory seem outworn symbols of a dead political fanaticism; for men of property it was enough to be a Pittite and an Englishman.

As the surge of life carried Pitt to the lonely symbolism of national consciousness and national destiny, he himself seemed more than ever unaware of the way the tide was setting. Inept, almost indifferent, in his handling of foreign affairs, Pitt alternately blustered and retreated. At Nootka Sound, in 1790, his threats of action caused the Spaniards to withdraw, and the Pacific coast was saved for Canada. The same technique against Catharine the Great over the question of Oshakov failed miserably. Both actions were unconnected with any general diplomatic scheme; they were the result of immediate decisions. But Pitt's incapacity to comprehend is most marked in his attitude to France. No man distrusted the Revolution more, and yet he steadily reduced our naval armament, and, in 1792, confidently predicted fifteen years of tranquillity and peace. But the French torrent rushed on: help was offered by them to all revolutionary movements; they tore up their treaty obligations and opened the Scheldt, which was an age-old threat to English commerce; finally they decapitated their King. Although Pitt would not openly join the Allies, he steadily rejected all overtures of republican France for an alliance. Realizing what must inevitably happen, the French, much to the joy of George III, declared war on Britain on 1 February 1793. Throughout the months of crisis Pitt's own actions and statements seemed to have little reference to the volcanic nature of events or to the inevitable consequences of his own resolution. He set the price which he was prepared to accept for peace and kept to it with supreme determination, but he was optimistically blind to the fact that France could never afford it. His arrogance was so great that he was unable to understand that it was impossible for a revolution to bow to his will. And yet that self-same arrogance was to carry him, and his country, through years of tribulation and defeat.

CHAPTER SEVEN

THE WAR AT SEA
1793–1802

PITT had become reconciled to a war with France only when France had violated the traditional commercial interests of England by opening the Scheldt and when, by her attack on Holland, we were committed by our Treaty obligations. His conception of the war was to check the increasing aggression of France. But this conception was too limited for George III, for Burke, and for an important section of the cabinet. They all wished to see not only France but the Revolution defeated, and the Bourbons restored. Subject as he was to royal, public, and political pressure, Pitt compromised, and his compromise was fatal for military success. He agreed to give help to subversive movements in France, but insisted also on fighting a war on the traditional lines of his father. His military resources were inadequate for either policy, but Pitt was supremely confident that the war would be short. In 1793 he increased neither taxation nor his armed forces.

As the year drew on Pitt's confidence seemed fully justified. When war broke out the French were about to overwhelm a defenceless and complaining Holland, but, as soon as the veteran Austrian troops under Coburg moved against their flanks, the attack collapsed. Retreat and recrimination followed until in disgust Dumouriez, the most accomplished of French generals, deserted to the Allies, taking his guest, the French Foreign Secretary, with him. The road to Paris was wide open: a royalist insurrection in La Vendée and the defection of Toulon, France's great Mediterranean naval base, made Allied victory seem a matter of weeks. So much so that Pitt agreed to the interventionist policy and diverted troops destined for the West Indies. But there was no agreement as to where they should go. Burke clamoured for support of the Vendeans: the navy insisted on the priority of Toulon. The troops went to aid the Duke of York in Flanders on what was expected to be his triumphal march on Paris.

But the weakness of France, so obvious to the Allies, was more apparent than real. In Paris the Committee of Public Safety, under the demonic leadership of Robespierre, was transforming French economy. The flamboyant use of the guillotine has distracted attention from the extraordinary efficiency of the Terror in mobilizing the industrial resources and manpower of France in a way which was novel to European society. Never before had the entire life of a nation been organized for war. This, backed by the inspiration of the Revolution, changed the French army from an officerless and disorderly rabble to the most efficient military machine the world had seen. But the Committee needed time; even the feverish energy of Carnot and Robespierre could accomplish little in weeks – they needed months. And months were given to them. The Allies moved with formal deliberation. Coburg, the Commander-in-Chief, insisted on reducing every point of resistance, big or small, and defending in depth every mile he gained. The Prussians, with Pitt's subsidy in their pockets, waited on the Rhine for the Austrian victory and discussed a further partition of Poland with the Russians. Unable to wait for the deferred victory, they began to despatch troops to the East, setting up such anxiety in the Austrian Command that they failed to keep their minds on the Western campaign. At first the French could only contain the Allies, but by the time winter put an end to war in Flanders almost the whole of Northern France was clear of the enemy and Robespierre and Carnot had the time which they needed. They devoted their energies to the South and East where war was possible. Toulon fell, and made the reputation of Bonaparte, who led the artillery. Alsace-Lorraine, the Palatinate, and Piedmont were all cleared in the months considered by Allied generals unfit for fighting. Even so, when the Flanders campaign opened again in April, the advantages were entirely with the Allies, for they possessed 160,000 seasoned troops against the newly-raised French conscripts. In spite of initial successes, the Austrians threw away immense advantages, and greater opportunities, by maintaining the solemn minuet of text-book tactics. The French acted with spectacular boldness. Gambling on Prussian immobility, they switched the army of the Rhine and threw it against the Austrian flank. Coburg was too learned a general not to appreciate the full strategic implications. He withdrew. A generation was to pass before Austrian and British troops were to meet again.

The British remained with the Dutch. They got behind the Waal and welcomed the winter mud. But winter played false. By January every river, ditch, and creek in Holland was frozen. And again the French violated the canons of military dogma and advanced. The result was harrowing disaster and defeat for the British army. Only a remnant escaped from Bremen in the spring. The war in the North was over. The Prussians made peace. The Batavian Republic replaced Holland and the Netherlands, and thus added immeasurably to French naval strength.

The policy of intervention in the continental war had ended in disaster. Pitt, however, had always been unconvinced that such a policy was in Britain's interest. He favoured his father's strategy – the use of seapower to collect the enemy's commercial empire. He had held troops from Toulon, from Vendée, from the Duke of York's armies, and sent them to the West Indies to collect the rich French sugar islands. But the sugar islands were not as easy to collect as they had been in the past. The principles of the French

Revolution – liberty, equality, fraternity – had been held out to the French slaves as an enticement to fight for their masters. They fought, and fought well. In such a climate a quick victory was essential, but the determination of the French black troops prevented it, and the British soldiers died in hundreds.* Pitt was not a man to withdraw to cut his losses, once a decision had been taken, and the West Indies continued to eat up the inadequate resources of the British army. Politically, for Pitt, the West Indies campaign was essential. He was strongly supported by West Indian interests, which coveted the French islands, and they were terrified at the possible growth and success of revolutionary ideas amongst the slaves. Defeat in Europe, disaster in the West Indies, bad harvests, and loss of markets – it was no wonder that discontent was rife at home. The mob broke Pitt's windows, revolutionary clubs multiplied, and Pitt began a policy of repression. Governing circles clutched eagerly at straws of hope and magnified immediately any action which had the appearance of victory. Howe's defeat of the French Fleet at Ushant (1 June 1794), an action of exceptional but misplaced bravery, was acclaimed with bonfires and bellringing, but the fact that a huge grain convoy got safely into Brest to relieve a starving France was ignored. The capture of Cape Town, Ceylon, and the East Indies, when Holland was overrun by the French, was used to appease the disappointments of the West Indies, and to diminish successful French intrigues with the Mahrattas in India. But Pitt needed no such straws. He faced the future with a lofty calm. Looking to 1795, he told the Commons:

It matters little whether the disasters which have arisen are to be ascribed to the weakness of generals, the intrigues of camps, or the jealousies of Cabinets; the fact is they exist, and that we must anew commence the salvation of Europe.

*Between 1794 and 1796, 40,000 British troops died in the West Indies.

The next two years were to tax Pitt's confidence and to drive him to a fruitless overture for peace. In 1795 France's position, although improved, was far from secure. Chronic inflation had brought misery and starvation which made the royalist outbreaks in the West more threatening. The Austrians counter-attacked with effect, clearing the French from the Palatinate, and driving them along the Riviera where they should have been joined by an amphibious British force from Corsica. No force arrived, for the essential British troops had been dissipated in a fruitless attempt to support royalists in the West, and to strengthen the depleted garrisons of the West Indies. British weakness was underlined when the French fleet escaped from Toulon and captured the entire Levant convoy, causing shivers of apprehension in the City. Infinitely worse was to follow. In 1796 Napoleon attacked the Austrian armies in Italy.

The advent of Napoleon transformed the war. The Terror had organized France for war more efficiently and more thoroughly than ever a State had been organized before, but the organization had been used to plunder the people of France. The bankers, contractors, and swindlers who controlled France under the Directory were uninterested in victory so long as the war continued at a safe distance from France's frontiers. Napoleon, with all the emotional ferocity and energy of genius, was single-minded for victory. In a brilliant campaign which established him as France's greatest general, he threw the Austrians out of Italy and had them suing for peace within a year. Napoleon's successes brought Spain openly on the side of France, and Britain's naval position seemed hopelessly compromised. We were forced to leave the Mediterranean. By the spring of 1797 Britain had no allies left on the Continent, for even Portugal had made peace with France. For the next eighteen months Britain was on the verge of defeat.

France planned to invade Britain. Ireland was seething with rebellion,* and an expedition of fifteen thousand men was organized under La Hoche to sail from Brest, whilst the Dutch fleet at Texel threatened the East coast. Gales and miscalculations saved Ireland, for nothing could have stopped Hoche's troops had they landed in Bantry Bay. Effrontery and guile kept the Dutch fleet in the Texel. With two ships only Duncan foxed the Dutch into believing that he had the whole fleet waiting beyond the horizon. In fact, the fleet was in mutiny at the Nore.

The mutinies at Spithead and the Nore from April to June 1797 mark the lowest ebb of Britain's fortunes. The condition of both the army and the navy was appalling; the floggings and the brutality horrified even eighteenth-century Prussians. Death by beating for quite trivial offences, such as drunkenness, caused scarcely a stir of conscience; food was always rotten, pay overdue and scanty, living conditions were unbearable. Promotion rarely went by merit; commissions were hawked for purchase; the financial resources of the armed forces were the object of deliberate and calculated plunder.† The professional soldier or sailor was inured to these degrading conditions but the new drafts who were pressed, or raised by the quota system, bitterly resented their new situation. Timely reforms by the Duke of York, an honest and able administrator, from 1795, probably prevented mutiny in what was left of the army after the West Indian campaigns. But in spite of ample warning nothing was done for the fleet. Both mutinies were completely free from any sympathy with the French, and at no time was there any danger of the ships deserting. The mutineers were emphatic in their intention to sail as soon as the French

*Cf. chapter five.

†Within a month of his appointment as Commander-in-Chief in 1795 the Duke of York had ordered a return of all captains under twelve and all lieutenant-colonels under twenty.

appeared. The Spithead mutiny was relatively a mild affair, settled satisfactorily by Howe, who promised to redress the all-too-obvious grievances. The Nore mutiny, under the determined and able leadership of Parker, was more serious. He demanded considerable democratization of the fleet and attempted to obtain his demands by threatening London. He failed and was hanged. But he had frightened the Admiralty, which slowly began to improve the conditions of service and to grant a great deal of what the mutineers had demanded.*

The mutinies were not the only tribulation which the British had to bear that summer; prices soared and throughout the country the poor verged on starvation. The whole financial structure of the country seemed to the common man to be on the point of collapse when the Bank of England suspended cash payments. Without allies, on the verge of rebellion, social anarchy, and bankruptcy, Pitt attempted to make peace on terms which were the acknowledgement of defeat, but they were not enough for the war party in France, and the attempt failed.

In the autumn of 1797 the tide turned. As the Dutch fleet emerged from the Texel, Duncan sailed his ships to leeward into shallow coastal water. It was an act of outrageous bravery, but Duncan wanted a decisive victory. He got it and, after Camperdown, the Dutch fleet no longer existed as a threat of invasion. Duncan's ships were the mutineers' ships from the Nore, and the victory of Camperdown was an immense relief to the public, and gave the navy itself a renewed and intense pride. But, more important still, Duncan's victory permitted new risks to be taken. The threat of an invasion across the Channel was diminished. Earlier in the year Jervis and Nelson had considerably damaged the Spanish fleet at Cape St Vincent. Under these

*The best account of the mutinies is to be found in *The Floating Republic* by G. E. Manwaring and Bonamy Dobrée. Pelican Books.

circumstances a decision was taken to re-enter the Mediterranean. Nelson commanded the fleet.

The story of the next few years is the story of Nelson, who became the enduring symbol of England's salvation through her supremacy at sea. Nelson, Norfolk born, had become a midshipman at twelve; from that time he loved the navy with a passion which was almost religious in its ardour. He longed for martyrdom in the drama of victory. No detail about his ships, or his men, was too petty for his lavish and insistent care; no danger too great for his ardent ambition.* He was an uncomfortable man for those in authority. His confident arrogance made him a difficult subordinate, and his conviction that he was a man of destiny infuriated lesser men. His infatuation for Lady Hamilton, and the ostentation of their relationship, provided excuses for those who distrusted and feared him. But for those who served him, and for the public, these things did not count. They remembered his reckless heroism, the way he had lost his eye doing the army's job in Corsica; or his mad attack on a treasure ship at Santa Cruz in which he had lost his right arm. His skill at St Vincent had shown that he was a great, as well as a brave, admiral. When he led the fleet back into the Mediterranean the British world knew that he would take every possible risk to bring the French fleet to battle, and that the battle would be decisive. He would destroy or be destroyed.

At first luck ran against Nelson. Napoleon with a formidable fleet slipped out of Toulon, eluded Nelson, and sailed East. Napoleon's destination was any man's guess – Italy, Malta, Egypt, Syria, Turkey. Malta was his first objective, but, quickly captured, it was quickly left. Nelson chased on to Alexandria to find the port unoccupied. He decided that Napoleon's destination was Syria. Two days after Nelson

*'In my mind's eye, I ever saw a radiant orb suspended which beckoned me onwards to renown.' (Nelson.)

had sailed, Napoleon landed unchallenged, and quickly conquered Lower Egypt. But Nelson returned again and discovered the French fleet in Aboukir Bay, close inshore. Without hesitation, Nelson sailed his fleet into the shoal water between the French and the land. Napoleon's navy was slaughtered, and the Mediterranean mastered. It was daring, heroic, devastating; a strategic victory won through the finest calculation of risk. For the rest of the war with Napoleon, we entered the Mediterranean at will.

The public at home received the news with almost idolatrous rapture, for the people of England knew at once that it meant survival, and the chance of victory. And this confidence was reinforced. At Acre a handful of British sailors, led by Sir Sidney Smith, held the French army in check whilst fever killed them. Encouraged, the powers of Europe formed the Second Coalition to force the French back into France, paid for by the subsidies raised by Pitt's latest and most daring financial innovation, the tax on incomes. At first the Second Coalition prospered. Suvorov, the great Russian general, recaptured Northern Italy, but the hopes so raised were quickly extinguished. Abandoning his army in Egypt, Napoleon eluded Nelson's watching frigates. Back in Paris, he cleared out the rotten Directorate which had battened on the war like flies on carrion. Calling himself 'First Consul', Napoleon assumed authoritarian control of France. Moving with the same confidence on land as Nelson did at sea, he quickly destroyed the armies of the Second Coalition. His crossing of the Great St Bernard to force a decisive victory at Marengo (1800) was of the same quality of fine, calculated risk as Nelson's at Aboukir. This battle and Moreau's victory at Hohenlinden forced Austria to peace (Lunéville, 1801). Already the Russians had deserted the coalition. The half-demented Tsar Paul had developed a passionate admiration for Napoleon, and conceived vast fantastic projects for the destruction of Britain and her

Empire; most were chimerical, but one, the Armed Neutrality, was a serious threat to our sea power.

The Armed Neutrality was a league of the Northern powers to prevent, by force of arms if necessary, the search by the British of neutral ships for contraband. In effect, this meant that war between Britain and the Northern powers was certain, and the broken French naval forces would be reinforced with a strong Danish fleet, and the Baltic with its precious naval supplies – pitch, hemp, pine – would be closed to us. Again it was Nelson, and again the same finely-calculated risk, the knife edge between victory and defeat, and this time defeat would have meant disgrace, for victory was won only by ignoring his superior officer's commands. But the victory was overwhelming, the Danish fleet was annihilated under the very eyes of the Danes. And then, as the British fleet sailed up the Baltic to deal with the Russians at Reval, they learned that Tsar Paul had been murdered by his own officers. The new Tsar, Alexander, did not want war. The Armed Neutrality was at an end, and the Baltic, as well as the Mediterranean, was free to British shipping.

Within two years, and by sea power alone, Britain had passed through the shadow of defeat. In 1798 Ireland was in revolt, the French were massed to invade, the navy was mutinous and unreliable, and there was nothing but half-trained, half-armed volunteers to match against the finest general and greatest army Europe had yet seen. In 1801 that general and that army were still unconquered. Europe was his, and it seemed to many that it always would be so. Perhaps, so long as we maintained the freedom of the seas and our wealth of colonies, it might be possible to live in amity with the French. So, when peace was offered, it was readily, too readily, accepted. The treaty of Amiens was signed in 1802, and Englishmen swarmed across the Channel; but the time for sight-seeing was short.

CHAPTER EIGHT

THE WAR ON LAND
1802–15

ONCE the sense of relief in being at peace had passed, all England realized that it was only a matter of months before the struggle was renewed. Napoleon had regarded the Treaty of Amiens as a new tactic in his struggle for Empire. This treaty had restored French possessions in the Caribbean; France possessed Louisiana; the vast hinterland was unclaimed, but a secret understanding with Spain allowed Napoleon to dream of a French Empire stretching from the Gulf of Mexico to the Golden Gate. But, even as he dreamed, his practised mind exploited the confusions of Europe to weaken still further Britain's position: with his grasp of military reality he knew that Britain must be conquered. Whilst Addington shillied and shallied, he took a firm grip on Switzerland, Holland, and Piedmont. When it was clear that public opinion would drive Addington willy-nilly into war, he sold Louisiana to the Americans, and tried to force England to evacuate Malta. The last was a misjudgement. After astonishing acts of appeasement the British government became stiff-necked about Malta, and Napoleon was at war sooner than he expected or wished, for much of his fleet was scattered in the Caribbean.

It was easier for the government to declare war than to fight it. Apart from the capture of a few French ships, the British could only wait on Napoleon's intentions, for his armies had swept through Italy, and we lacked allies. It was not long before his intentions disclosed themselves – the invasion of England; every port in Europe was rushed into a frenzy of shipbuilding: the Grand Army was brought to the Pas de Calais. The British government, short of troops, called for volunteers, and the response was an outburst of military fervour which astonished and delighted the nation. Nearly half a million men joined their local Volunteer Associations within a few months and the government was forced to stop recruiting. The patriots provided themselves with splendid regimentals, but arms were so short that pikes were distributed. As the weeks passed, contradictory and confusing orders were issued from Whitehall; in spite of a frenzied and vitriolic campaign of abuse and fear, fervour died, and frustration grew, as Napoleon failed to appear. In the alarms and fears and confusions Addington and his government cut a sorry figure; the demand for the return of Pitt grew overwhelming, but personal spite and factional jealousy prevented a national government under his leadership. Weak as his ministry was, and though he himself was broken in health, he assumed office, much to the relief of the nation. His policy was threefold: to maintain our power at sea; to organize defence in depth; to resuscitate a European Coalition. The last two required time, and Napoleon retained the initiative.

Napoleon had both ships and men:* there were times which favoured him, when the Channel was at his mercy. Each time the decisive act was deferred. So long as Napoleon's army was in being he knew that France would rule Europe, but flung into England, checked there, and hampered by the Fleet – what then? Unlike a battle, the decision could not be instinctive, the reflex of challenge and danger; it became a calculation of chances, of contingencies, inflated with responsive anxiety. The decision was taken to diminish the risk by luring the British fleet from the protection of the Channel, not for days, but for weeks.

*British naval historians doubt whether his shipping was sufficient: such calculations are almost impossible, and the French acted as if they had enough.

In spite of the Martello towers, the canals, the ditches, and the entrenchments, and notwithstanding the increased efficiency of the volunteers due to Pitt's prompt actions, it had always been understood that the safety of the country depended on the navy. As soon as war had broken out again the fleets had taken up their old blockading stations to keep once more the Mediterranean and Atlantic fleets of France apart, and to prevent their union with the Spanish. For eighteen months Nelson had patrolled the Gulf of Lions, whilst Cornwallis had watched and protected the Channel. Early in 1805 the situation changed dramatically. Villeneuve slipped out of Toulon, eluded Nelson's frigates, collected the Spanish fleet in Cadiz, and disappeared into the Atlantic. Nelson chased Villeneuve to the West Indies and back again. The Admiralty, forewarned by Nelson, sent a fleet under Calder to effect an interception which took place off Cape Finisterre. Villeneuve slipped into Corunna. Nelson joined Cornwallis off Brest. The opportunity for a decisive sea battle at the entrance to the Channel existed. Villeneuve declined and retreated to Cadiz. Napoleon's scheme to delude the British fleet, control the Channel, and invade failed. He was well aware of this before Villeneuve had turned south to Cadiz: he had been moving the Grand Army eastward to deal with the menace of the Third Coalition which Pitt's diplomacy had raised.

The struggle at sea was not over. In September Nelson went south to join the waiting fleet off Cadiz. He was resolved to destroy the French and Spanish fleets, and for the purpose he had evolved new naval tactics. Catching the enemy fleet off Cape Trafalgar on 21 October 1805, he sailed at them in two columns to break their line in two places. Bewildered and outmanoeuvred, the enemy was annihilated. In the midst of battle Nelson's chest was shattered; he died slowly in great agony but with the knowledge that his achievement was final – the martyrdom, long and heroically sought, completed. Safe from invasion, England was too stunned by its loss to rejoice. In the long years of war Nelson had been a fixed star of bravery and endurance.

To Napoleon, at the time, Trafalgar was an acute irritant rather than a disaster, for his preoccupations had become European. Before the news of the defeat reached him he had outwitted the Austrians under Mack at Ulm; six weeks later he crushingly defeated them with the Russians at Austerlitz. The Third Coalition was broken. It was in this atmosphere of disaster and defeat that Pitt had died on 23 January 1806. The country paid his debts and buried him by his father in Westminster Abbey. He was forty-six, a strange, powerful, desolate character. No politician is so difficult to assess. The other two great politicians of the eighteenth century, Walpole and Chatham, offer few problems either in their temperaments or in their achievements. In both Pitt is an enigma. He was a great orator; a dexterous and astute parliamentary politician, but without Walpole's humanity; his approach to the critical problems of his time was always narrowly rational, and frequently mistaken; a sound administrator; atrociously bad in all questions of strategy; with astonishing strength and persistence of will; a drunkard. Yet his nature and abilities are so twisted into the fabric of our history that this age of war is peculiarly his: more than any other man, far more than Burke, he riveted the new, emerging world of nineteenth-century England to the country's past, to its tradition, and to its history.

Pitt dead, a ministry of all talents and all factions was possible and the King reluctantly agreed to accept the detested Fox, who emerged, at death's door, from his long sojourn in the wilderness. He knew that he had only months to live, and he worked for the two objects which he had always prized – peace and the abolition of the inhumanity of the slave trade. Before he died he knew that in the latter

he had been successful, and the trade was abolished from
1 January 1808, but his search for peace was a failure.
Napoleon had no need for peace, but he was prepared to
negotiate while he rearranged Europe to his satisfaction.
He appropriated territories for his brothers. Joseph was
given Italy; Louis, Holland. Finally, Napoleon smashed
what was left of the coalition at Jena, Auerstadt, and Fried-
land. Prussia was dismembered. The Tsar made peace at
Tilsit. And Napoleon's plan for defeating England without
invasion was soon complete and crystal-clear. The Continent
was to be closed to British trade. Denmark, Sweden, and
Portugal were, if necessary, to be coerced. For the first time
in the history of Europe economic warfare on the grand scale
was attempted. By a series of decrees all British and Colonial
trade was excluded from Europe, and non-adherence to this
system was regarded by Napoleon as a just cause of war.
Having given up the project of invasion, it was the only
scheme which promised any success, but, to obtain it, Napoleon demanded a degree of self-sacrifice from his satellite
kingdoms which they were not prepared to make. He lacked
the administrative machinery and techniques to enforce his
continental system on unwilling partners. From the very
start there was smuggling and connivance on a scale large
enough to hamstring the system.

England attempted retaliation. French sea-borne trade
was stopped; all neutral shipping was prevented from trading with all adherents of the Continental System. The
right of search, which we enforced rigorously, precipitated
a war between ourselves and the United States, and our
economy was disturbed as much by our Orders in Council
as by Napoleon's Decrees. The years 1807 to 1810 were years
of great hardship and peril. Had Napoleon been able to enforce his system he might easily have won; had he forbidden
exports from, as well as imports to, Europe, especially grain
in the famine years 1809–12, he certainly would have done so.

Fortunately the art of economic warfare was in its infancy, and Napoleon had the unshakable belief that a threat to the pocket of a shopkeeper was more vital than a blow at his belly. Even so, the hardship inflicted was grievous; starvation was rife, and at Manchester dragoons had to be used to disperse desperate weavers on the point of rebellion.

In order to make his blockade thoroughly efficacious, Napoleon was forced to secure the adherence of Spain and Portugal to the Continental System, especially Portugal, which maintained special economic ties with Great Britain. He ordered Spain to help him drive out the Portuguese royal family and to partition Portugal. To do so he poured troops into Spain; once there the Bourbon royal family was turned out, and his brother Joseph promoted from the kingdom of Italy to the throne of Spain. On 2 May 1808 the Spanish people rose in revolt, murdered what Frenchmen they could lay hands on, and sent a hurried deputation to demand help from England.

Canning, the new Foreign Secretary, did not hesitate. By the end of July British troops under Sir Arthur Wellesley, afterwards the Duke of Wellington, had landed at the mouth of the Tagus. British troops never again quitted the Continent until the defeat of Napoleon seven years later at Waterloo. Wellington was confident that he could beat the French armies.

It's enough to make one thoughtful [he said shortly after his appointment]. But no matter. My die is cast: they may overwhelm me, but I don't think they will out-manoeuvre me. First, because I am not afraid of them, as everyone else seems to be; secondly, because, if what I hear of their system of manoeuvres be true, I think it is a false one against steady troops. I suspect that all the Continental armies were more than half beaten before the battle was begun. I, at least, will not be frightened beforehand.

Of Wellington's genius there is no question, but it needed more than genius to defeat Napoleon. It required an

army. During the long years of war the British army had
experienced defeat and disaster, but its quality had steadily
improved. The Duke of York had improved immeasurably
the administration and supply, and Sir John Moore at
Shorncliffe had created a well disciplined and superbly
equipped body of light infantry – troops peculiarly well
suited to the immense distances and mountainous country
of Spain.

No sooner had Wellington landed in Spain than he was
superseded in his command on the very day of the first
successful battle at Vimeiro when the British broke the
French troops under Junot. A major blunder followed. By
the Convention of Cintra Junot was allowed to withdraw
with his troops from Portugal. The outcry at home was so
violent that a court martial followed. Although Wellington
was completely exonerated, the command of British troops
in Spain was given not to him but to Sir John Moore.

Sir John Moore's campaign in the peninsula captured the
imagination of generations of Englishmen because of its
David and Goliath quality. The recent defeats by Spanish
and British troops had offended French susceptibility, and
Napoleon also realized the danger of successful military
action by his enemies in Portugal to his whole Continental
System. He resolved to settle the matter himself. Having
entered Spain, Napoleon crushed Spanish resistance, and
entered Madrid, when Moore, feeling his way forward,
reached Salamanca. Instead of abandoning his allies, and
falling back to defend Lisbon, Moore struck north to cut
Napoleon's communications. Realizing his danger, Napoleon turned to attack Moore, who retreated rapidly towards
the coast. In one delaying action at Benavente, and again at
Corunna, the British troops showed that Vimeiro had not
been a flash in the pan, and that they possessed sufficient
fighting qualities and discipline to match the French. When
it was obvious that Moore might escape, Napoleon had

given the command to Soult and left Spain. The retreat to
Corunna saved Portugal and Spain, although it cost valuable troops and Moore's own life. At his death the command
passed to Wellington.

For the next four years the Peninsular war was fought in
curious isolation. It bore little relation to the general diplomatic or military concentrations against Napoleon; at home
many leading politicians wished to see the army withdrawn
in time to cut what they considered to be inevitable losses.
The result was half-hearted support in men and materials
for Wellington and disastrous diversions of the army effort,
as at Walcheren and in Italy. Wellington carefully prepared
unassailable lines at Torres Vedras across the peninsula
upon which Lisbon was situated. This was to be his ultimate
fortress behind which he retreated when the French appeared in overwhelming strength under Masséna, who at
once realized their impregnable quality. But he failed to
realize the heroic quality of the Portuguese peasantry, who
left him with a waste land, or the quality of the British-
drilled Portuguese troops who harassed the besieging French.
In the end the French were forced to retreat, and then the
magnificent generalship of Wellington and the flexible
fighting qualities of his light infantry were displayed. At
Ciudad Rodrigo and Fuentes d'Onoro he repeated the
brilliant victories of the previous year. When, in October
1811, the armies went into winter quarters, Wellington had
fallen back once more to the Portuguese border, but Napoleon's marshals dared not press him back to Torres Vedras.
The summer of 1812 saw similar campaigns. Twice the
French were heavily defeated at Ciudad Rodrigo and at
Badajoz, and then Wellington fell back on Portugal in face
of superior forces, but with his army intact, so preventing
Napoleon withdrawing troops which were so desperately
needed elsewhere.

For 1812 had witnessed the turn of the tide. The uneasy

alliance with Russia, forged at Tilsit, had snapped, and the furious Napoleon had plunged into Russia to teach the Tsar a lesson, only to learn one himself. By luck, he escaped annihilation and capture, but not defeat, and this defeat came at a time when Prussia had acquired the means to take revenge for the humiliations which the country had suffered after Tilsit. Austria, in spite of her recent dynastic ties with Napoleon, prepared for war. Metternich offered armed mediation, but Napoleon, determined to punish Russia and Prussia utterly and thoroughly, rejected them. The next year disaster followed defeat. At Leipzig the combined armies of the Fourth Coalition crushed the French. The road to France was open, and the brilliant defensive tactics of Napoleon could only postpone, and not prevent, the Allies' march to Paris. The necessities of his German campaign had led Napoleon to weaken his Spanish armies; whereas Wellington's victories, and the retreat from Moscow, had made the Peninsular war popular for the first time with the British, and men and supplies had been sent out to strengthen Wellington. Within forty days of the opening of the campaign, the French army had been routed at Vitoria, and the British army was poised, ready to invade France across the Pyrenees. After twenty years of almost constant warfare, the French attempt to dominate Europe was at an end, and peace at hand. Before it was achieved both the British army and Wellington were called upon to secure what Europe had won. Escaping from Elba, where the European powers, assembled in Congress at Vienna, had imprisoned him, Napoleon had raised a dejected and disgruntled France, driven out the Bourbons, and made a bid for European power. He had driven his army up into Belgium in a hope of cutting off the British from the Central European powers, and on 18 June 1815 one of the most decisive battles of modern Europe was fought at Waterloo. In Wellington's words it was 'a damned nice thing', but his thin red line held, and he was not outmanoeuvred. The appearance of a fresh Prussian army under Blücher at the end of the battle turned defeat to a rout.

After twenty years of war Great Britain had emerged the strongest, richest, and most powerful country in the world. Any demands which she might have made must have been met by the Congress of Vienna. She made very few; a strategic trading port here and there, Malta, Mauritius, the Cape, Ceylon – to secure her sea-borne wealth. And yet it was not complacency with regard to her future which narrowed her demands, but rather a sense of the overwhelming difficulties which she faced, and the burden of her obligations which would bear no extension. The war and the Continental System had aggravated the confusions and social disasters of rapid industrial change. In 1815 Great Britain seemed on the edge of bankruptcy and social revolution. Starvation was driving the poor to wreck the machinery which seemed to them to be the cause of the misery, and the government, without wisdom and without foresight, repressed brutally what in its turn it could not comprehend. To thinking men the horizon was dark and foreboding. After a century of war France had been defeated in the struggle for commercial empire, and at last the ports of the New World were open. India was ours. But what a racked and distracted Britain might make of these long-sought opportunities was hidden in the future; in 1815, at the end of long endurance, there was fear, and envy, and greed, but little hope.

FURTHER READING LIST

THE best bibliography of English eighteenth-century history is Stanley Pargellis and D. J. Medley, *Bibliography of British History. The Eighteenth Century 1714–1789* (1951). For the period 1789–1815 students should consult the *Subject Index of the London Library* (1909, 1923, 1938). Admirable collections of source material, with expert commentary and full bibliographies, may be found in *English Historical Documents* Vol. X ed. by D. B. Horn and Mary Ransome (1957) and Vol. XI ed. by A. A. Aspinall and E. A. Smith (1959).

The best general history of the period still is W. E. H. Lecky's *History of England in the Eighteenth Century* (Cabinet edition, 1899–1901), in spite of its strong Whig bias and its shortcomings in economic history. The two volumes devoted to this period in *The Oxford History of England* are more factually accurate and more up-to-date in interpretation. The better of the two is undoubtedly Steven Watson's *The Reign of George III* (1960), a remarkable summary of a difficult period: the less good, but much improved by Charles Stuart in the revised edition (1961), is Basil Williams' *The Whig Supremacy*. A shorter introduction is provided by J. H. Plumb, *The First Four Georges* (1956), but by far the best brief survey is to be found in the chapter, 'The Historical Background', in Vol. X of Sir William Holdsworth's *History of English Law* (1938), a masterpiece in miniature, buried in this vast and important work.

Since Arnold Toynbee published his *Lectures on the Industrial Revolution in England* (1884) generations of scholars have devoted themselves to the elucidation of the problems caused by the rapid changes in English social and economic life of the eighteenth century. Fortunately Professor T. S. Ashton has summarized a lifetime's study and research in his *Industrial Revolution* (1948) and *An Economic History of England, the Eighteenth Century* (1955), books of rare insight and profound learning. *The Industrial Revolution, a Study in Bibliography* (1937), also by Professor Ashton, is an indispensable guide to the immense literature of the subject. Other excellent surveys have been written by C. R. Fay, *Great Britain from Adam Smith to the Present Day* (1928), H. L. Beales, *The Industrial Revolution* (1928), A. Redford, *The Economic History of England, 1760–1860* (1931), and a longer and more detailed treatment is provided by the great French scholar Paul Mantoux, *The Industrial Revolution in the Eighteenth Century* (1928). In some ways the most attractive way of studying the Industrial Revolution is through local histories. Of these there are a great number, and Professor Ashton's advice should be followed, but there are two so outstanding as to demand special mention: J. D. Chambers, *Nottinghamshire in the Eighteenth Century* (1932), and W. H. B. Court, *The Rise of Midland Industries, 1600–1838* (1938). The difficulties inherent in any discussion of the origin and effects of the Industrial Revolution are brilliantly demonstrated in J. D. Chambers *The Vale of Trent* (n.d.).

The social history of the eighteenth century has received perhaps less attention than the economic, but, even so, the literature is vast. The best introduction is Chapters X–XVI of G. M. Trevelyan's *Social History* (1944), one of the finest pieces of historical writing of our time. A more detailed treatment will be found in *Johnson's England* (1933), ed. A. S. Turberville. Other books of great value are: M. Dorothy George, *London Life in the XVIIIth Century* (1925), *England in Transition* (Penguin Books, 1953); Dorothy Marshall, *English People in the Eighteenth Century* (1956); E. Neville Williams, *Life in Georgian England* (1962); G. D. H. Cole and Raymond Postgate, *The Common People, 1746–1938* (1938); Gladys M. Jones, *The Charity School Movement in the XVIIIth Century* (1938), a delightful book which illuminates many neglected aspects of eighteenth-century life. Sidney and Beatrice Webb provided an inexhaustible mine for social historians in their monumental work on *English Local Government*, 7 vols. (1906–29), a book which can be read for an hour or for weeks with equal pleasure and benefit.

The constitutional, political, and religious history of the century is steadily being cleared of the misconceptions of nineteenth-century historians. The true nature of eighteenth-century politics has been brilliantly described by Professor L. B. Namier in two books, *The Structure of Politics at the Accession of George III* (2nd ed. 1957) and *England in the Age of the American Revolution* (2nd ed. 1962). A fine recent study of the complicated constitutional problems of this difficult period has been made by R. Pares, *King George III and the Politicians* (1953). For the earlier period there is J. H. Plumb's biography of Sir Robert Walpole: Vol. I, *The Making of a Statesman* (1956) and Vol. II, *The King's Minister* (1960) which deal with the political and constitutional issues to 1734. Professor Norman Sykes, *Church and State in the XVIIIth Century* (1934), has done much to clear the eighteenth-century clergy from charges of idleness and corruption, and Professor H. Butterfield in *George III, Lord North and the People* (1950) has shown how constitutional, political, and social history can be combined to achieve the reconstruction of a great crisis in our history. The structure of politics of the eighteenth century has been the object of detailed study by a number of young scholars, using the methods of Sir Lewis Namier. The most important of these are: John B. Owen, *The Rise of the Pelhams* (1957); John Brooke, *The Chatham Administration* (1956); I. R. Christie, *The End of North's Ministry* (1958). A work of equal power, and in some ways of greater originality, is George Rudé, *Wilkes and Liberty* (1962). E. Neville Williams, *The Eighteenth Century Constitution* (1960) is an indispensable source book for political and constitutional history, made even more valuable by its excellent commentary.

The dramatic nature of England's imperial expansion has inspired some very fine historical writing, and a full bibliography is given in Vol. I of the *Cambridge History of the British Empire* (1929). It is difficult to select, but here are a few that I have found interesting and illuminating: Kate Hotblack, *Chatham's Colonial Policy* (1917), a rare, neglected book of great importance; J. A. Williamson, *The Ocean in English History* (1941), and the same author's *Cook and the Opening of the Pacific* (1946), which should be read with Cook's own account of his voyages (an admirable selection has been made recently by Christopher Lloyd, *Voyages of Captain Cook*, (1950); Vincent T. Harlow, *The Founding of the Second British Empire* (1952); Edward Thompson and G. T. Garratt, *The Rise and Fulfilment of British Rule in India* (1934); C. Northcote Parkinson, *Trade in the Eastern Seas* (1938), and *Trade Winds* (1948), ed. by the same author; Alfred Spencer (ed.), *Memoirs of William Hickey* (1913); J. C. Miller, *Origins of the American Revolution* (1945); C. M. Andrews, *The Colonial Background of the American Revolution* (1924); J. R. Alden, *The American Revolution* (1954).

The importance of the eighteenth century in the development of art, science, and thought has long been recognized, but Basil Willey's *The Eighteenth Century Background* (1940) breaks new ground; it is an essential book for the understanding of the cultural history of the period. Eighteenth-century literature has been the object of specialized attention, and for the best editions of authors, biographies, and criticism the student is advised to consult the bibliographies in Vols. IX, X, XI of the *Cambridge History of English Literature*, but Ian Watt's *The Rise of the Novel* (1957) is of exceptional interest for social historians of the period. For those who wish for a more detailed treatment of the history of philosophy, there is Sir Leslie Stephen's *History of English Thought in the Eighteenth Century* (1902); for the visual arts, Christopher Hussey, *The Picturesque* (1927), Professor A. E. Richardson, *An Introduction to Georgian Architecture* (1949), James Lees Milne, *The Age of Adam* (1947), John

Fleming, *Robert Adam and his Circle* (1962), John Rothenstein, *An Introduction to English Painting* (1933), and the very valuable series, *The Library of English Art*, ed. C. M. Weekley; for science there is Wolf, *A History of Science, Technology and Philosophy in the Eighteenth Century* (1938); for music P. A. Scholes, *History of Music* (6th ed. 1943), and his fascinating biography, *The Great Dr Burney*, 2 vols. (1948).

The narrow world of eighteenth-century politics and social life, with its scandals and intrigues, gave an added zest to the writing of letters and memoirs which have provided an inexhaustible quarry for the political biographers. No one has been more frequently used than Horace Walpole, who deliberately set out to portray his age; R. W. Ketton-Cremer, *Horace Walpole* (1939), is the best guide to his life and works. The best edition of Walpole's correspondence is that in process of publication by the Yale University Press under the general editorship of W. S. Lewis, but Mrs Paget Toynbee's edition of Walpole's letters (1903–5) will remain invaluable until this is completed. In the same class as Horace Walpole is John, Lord Hervey, *Memoirs of the Reign of King George II*, ed. Romney Sedgwick, 3 vols. (1931), the most vivid picture we have of life at an English Court.

Of biographies, there are legion; the greatest, of course, is Boswell's *Life of Johnson*, the best edition of which is G. Birkbeck Hill's. Of the rest, the following is a selection: Norman Sykes, *Edmund Gibson* (1926); C. H. and Muriel I. Baker's *James Brydges, First Duke of Chandos* (1949); Peter Quennell, *Caroline of England* (1939); Basil Williams, *Carteret and Newcastle* (1943); Basil Williams, *William Pitt, Earl of Chatham*, 2 vols. (1915); B. Tunstall, *William Pitt, Earl of Chatham* (1938); J. H. Plumb, *Chatham* (1953); Elsie Harrison, *Son to Susannah* (Penguin Books, 1945); John Steegman, *Sir Joshua Reynolds* (1938); J. T. Smith, *Nollekens and His Times* (World's Classics, 1929); Sir Philip Magnus, *Edmund Burke* (1939); Sir Reginald Coupland, *Wilberforce* (1923); J. Holland Rose, *William Pitt*, 2 vols. (1911); Christopher Hobhouse, *Fox* (1934); Raymond Postgate, *That Devil Wilkes* (1930); Hugh Carrington, *Captain Cook* (1939); Carola Oman, *Nelson* (1947); Samuel Smiles, *Lives of the Engineers* (1861–62); T. H. Marshall, *James Watt, 1736–1819* (1925); J. L. Clifford, *The Young Samuel Johnson* (1955); John W. Derry, *William Pitt* (1962); V. H. H. Green, *The Young Mr Wesley* (1961); Oliver Warner, *William Wilberforce* (1962); R. W. Ketton-Cremer, *Thomas Gray* (1955); R. Halsband, *Life of Lady Mary Wortley Montagu* (1956).

INDEX